Munro

Munro bagging is a popular activity in
enthusiasts to climb any of the 282 mc
high. To bag a Munro is the achieveme   ......g the top & therefore
being able to tick it off your list. Munroists or compleatists are people who
have climbed all 282 Munros so far, which is just over 6,000 people to date.
This is a great journal for anyone who wants to take on the challenge to
climb as many of the peaks during their lifetime!

This log book & journal is a perfect companion for anyone who loves the
challenging & thrilling activity of Munro Bagging. This journal includes a
page for each of the 282 Munros for you to record every detail of your walk
with space for notes & photos. It's organised in height ascending order &
includes a grid reference for each location. It's a great way to record all
your Munro adventures that you can treasure for years to come.

Please note:
Whether you're an experienced walker or an amateur it's your responsibility
to properly prepare before attempting any of these mountains. Good
preparation includes navigation skills by using a map & compass, hill craft
& prior experience before attempting these mountains. In case of
emergencies it's crucial that you take precaution before your trip and make
a note of any emergency contact information & the nearest mountain rescue
location.

Message from the author:
Thank you for choosing this book as your go to journal for Munro bagging.
I hope it's the perfect companion during your Munro adventures as it was
for me!

As a small author on Amazon, it's a joy to provide as much value to people
who enjoy the same passions as me & it's really appreciated when you
decide to buy one of my books. If this log book & journal comes in handy
during your travels I would really appreciate if you could kindly leave an
honest review on Amazon as this really helps a small author like me!

I wish you many joyous Munro bagging adventures!

- John Backpackers Publishing

List of Munros In Height Ascending Order:

1. Ben Vane (915m)
2. Beinn Teallach (915m)
3. Beinn a' Chleibh (916m)
4. Geal-Charn (917m)
5. Càrn Aosda (917m)
6. Sgùrr a' Mhadaidh (918m)
7. Ruadh Stac Mor (918m)
8. Meall na Teanga (918m)
9. Creag nan Damh (918m)
10. A'Ghlas-Bheinn (918m)
11. Gairich (919m)
12. Carn Sgulain (920m)
13. Sgiath Chùil (921m)
14. An Socach (921m)
15. Tom na Gruagaich (Beinn Alligin) (922m)
16. Sgùrr nan Each (923m)
17. An Coileachan (923m)
18. Sgùrr nan Eag (924m)
19. Creag Pitridh (924m)
20. Stob Coire Raineach (925m)
21. Seana Bhraigh (926m)
22. Meall a'Choire Leith (926m)
23. Geal Charn (926m)
24. Eididh nan Clach Geala (926m)
25. Beinn Liath Mhor (926m)
26. Beinn Narnain (927m)
27. Ben Hope (927m)
28. Bla Bheinn (Blabheinn) (928m)
29. Mayar (928m)
30. Meall nan Eun (928m)
31. Moruisg (928m)
32. A'Chailleach (930m)
33. Beinn Bhreac (931m)
34. Ben Chonzie (931m)
35. Meall Buidhe (932m)
36. Beinn Chabhair (933m)
37. Fionn Bheinn (933m)
38. Maol Chean-dearg (933m)
39. The Cairnwell (933m)
40. Am Basteir (934m)
41. Meall a'Chrasgaidh (934m)
42. Beinn na Lap (936m)
43. Beinn Sgulaird (937m)
44. Beinn Tarsuinn (937m)
45. Sron a'Choire Ghairbh (937m)
46. A'Bhuidheanach Bheag (937m)
47. Luinne Bheinn (939m)
48. Mount Keen (939m)
49. Mullach nan Coirean (939m)
50. Beinn a'Chroin (940m)
51. Carn Dearg (941m)
52. Carn na Caim (941m)
53. Ben Vorlich (943m)
54. Binnein Beag (943m)
55. An Socach (944m)
56. Sgurr Dubh Mor (944m)
57. Sgurr na Sgine (945m)
58. Bidein a'Choire Sheasgaich (945m)
59. Carn Dearg (945m)
60. Stob a'Choire Odhair (945m)
61. Beinn Tulaichean (946m)
62. Carn Bhac (946m)
63. Meall Buidhe (946m)
64. Creag a'Mhaim (947m)
65. Driesh (947m)
66. Beinn Bhuidhe (948m)
67. Sgurr Mhic Choinnich (948m)
68. Meall Gorm (949m)
69. Meall Chuaich (951m)
70. Beinn Mhanach (953m)
71. Aonach Eagach - Meall Dearg (953m)
72. Sgurr nan Coireachan (953m)
73. Beinn Liath Mhor Fannaich (954m)
74. Am Faochagach (954m)
75. Sgor Gaibhre (955m)
76. Buachaille Etive Mor - Stob na Broige (956m)
77. Saileag (956m)
78. Sgurr nan Coireachan (956m)
79. Carn Ghluasaid (957m)
80. Tom Buidhe (957m)
81. Bruach na Frithe (958m)
82. Buachaille Etive Beag - Stob Dubh (958m)
83. Tolmount (958m)
84. Beinn Fhionnlaidh (959m)
85. Meall Glas (959m)
86. Beinn nan Aighenan (960m)
87. Stuchd an Lochain (960m)
88. Sgorr Ruadh (961m)
89. Ben Khibreck - Meall nan Con (962m)
90. Carn a'Chlamain (963m)
91. Sgurr Thuilm (963m)
92. Sgurr nan Gillean (964m)
93. Sgurr na Banachdich (965m)
94. Ben More (966m)
95. A'Mhaighdean (967m)
96. Aonach Eagach - Sgorr nam Fiannaidh (967m)
97. Meall Garbh (968m)
98. Sgurr a'Ghreadaidh (972m)
99. Ben Lomond (973m)
100. Stuc a'Chroin (974m)
101. Beinn Sgritheall (974m)
102. Stob Ban (975m)
103. A'Mharconaich (975m)
104. Carn a'Gheoidh (975m)
105. Beinn a'Ghlo - Carn Liath (975m)
106. Cona' Mheall (977m)
107. Meall nan Ceapraichean (977m)
108. Stob Coire Sgriodain (978m)
109. Beinn Dubhchraig (978m)
110. Beinn a'Chochuill (979m)
111. Ciste Dhubh (979m)
112. Stob Coire a'Chairn (980m)
113. Mullach na Dheiragain (981m)
114. Maol Chinn-dearg (981m)
115. Meall na Aighean (981m)
116. Slioch (981m)
117. Ben Vorlich (982m)
118. An Gearanach (982m)
119. Sgurr Dearg - Inaccessible Pinnacle (985m)
120. Gulvain (Gaor Bheinn) (986m)
121. Beinn Alligin - Sgurr Mhor (986m)
122. Lurg Mhor (986m)
123. Sgurr Ban (987m)
124. Conival (987m)
125. Creag Leacach (987m)
126. Druim Shionnach (987m)
127. Sgairneach Mhor (989m)
128. Beinn Eunaich (989m)
129. Sgurr Alasdair (991m)
130. Sgurr na Ruaidhe (992m)
131. Carn nan Gobhar (992m)
132. Carn nan Gobhar (992m)
133. Beinn Eighe - Spidean Coire nan Clach (993m)
134. Carn an Fhidhleir [Carn Ealar] (994m)
135. Sgor dha n-Ulaidh (994m)
136. An Caisteal (995m)
137. Spidean Mialach (996m)
138. A'Chailleach (997m)
139. Glas Bheinn Mhor (997m)
140. Ben More Assynt (998m)
141. Broad Cairn (998m)
142. Stob Daimh [Stob Diamh] (998m)
143. Sgurr Breac (999m)
144. Sgurr Choinnich (999m)
145. Stob Ban (999m)
146. Aonach Meadhoin (1001m)
147. Beinn a'Bheithir - Sgorr Dhonuill (1001m)
148. Meall Greigh (1001m)
149. Sail Chaorainn [Sail Chaoruinn] (1002m)
150. Sgurr na Carnach (1002m)
151. Sgurr Mor (1003m)
152. Beinn an Dothaidh (1004m)
153. Sgurr an Lochain (1004m)
154. The Devil's Point (1004m)
155. Beinn Fhionnlaidh (1005m)
156. An Sgarsoch (1006m)
157. Carn Liath (1006m)
158. Maoile Lunndaidh 1007m)
159. Beinn Dearg (1008m)
160. Beinn Udlamain (1010m)
161. Beinn Eighe - Ruadh-stac Mor (1010m)
162. Sgurr an Doire Leathain (1010m)
163. Sgurr Eilde Mor (1010m)
164. The Saddle (1010m)
165. Beinn Ime (1011m)
166. Cairn Bannoch (1012m)
167. Garbh Chioch Mhor (1013m)
168. Beinn Bheoil (1019m)
169. Carn an Tuirc (1019m)
170. Mullach Clach a'Bhlair (1019m)

171. Mullach Coire Mhic Fhearchair (1019m)
172. Ladhar Bheinn (1020m)
173. Buachaille Etive Mor - Stob Dearg (1021m)
174. Aonach air Chrith (1022m)
175. Liathach - Mullach an Rathain (1023m)
176. Beinn a'Bheithir - Sgorr Dhearg (1024m)
177. Ben Challum [Beinn Chalhuim] (1025m)
178. Sgurr a'Mhaoraich (1027m)
179. Sgurr na Ciste Duibhe (1027m)
180. Ben Oss (1029m)
181. Carn an Righ (1029m)
182. Carn Gorm (1029m)
183. Am Bodach (1032m)
184. Beinn Fhada (1032m)
185. Carn Dearg (1034m)
186. Gleouraich (1035m)
187. Sgurr a'Bhealaich Dheirg (1036m)
188. Carn a'Mhaim (1037m)
189. Beinn Achaladair (1038m)
190. Meall Ghaordaidh (1039m)
191. Sgurr na Ciche (1040m)
192. Carn Mairg (1042m)
193. Meall nan Tarmachan (1044m)
194. Stob Coir' an Albannaich (1044m)
195. Beinn Iutharn Mhor (1045m)
196. Ben Wyvis - Glas Leathad Mor (1046m)
197. Chno Dearg (1046m)
198. Cruach Ardrain (1046m)
199. Carn an t-Sagairt Mor (1047m)
200. Creag Mhor (1047m)
201. Geal Charn (1049m)
202. Sgurr Fhuar-thuill (1049m)
203. Beinn a'Chaorainn (1050m)
204. Glas Tulaichean (1051m)
205. Sgurr a'Chaorachain (1053m)
206. Stob Poite Coire Ardair (1054m)
207. Toll Creagach (1054m)
208. Liathach - Spidean a'Choire Leith (1055m)
209. Na Gruagaichean (1056m)
210. An Teallach - Sgurr Fiona (1060m)
211. An Teallach - Bidein a'Ghlas Thuill (1062m)
212. Cairn of Claise (1064m)
213. Sgurr Fhuaran (1067m)
214. Glas Maol (1068m)
215. An Socach (1069m)
216. Meall Corranaich (1069m)
217. Beinn a'Ghlo - Braigh Coire Chruinn-bhalgain (1070m)
218. Stob Coire Sgreamhach (1072m)
219. Beinn Dorain (1076m)
220. Beinn Heasgarnich [Beinn Sheasgarnaich] (1078m)
221. Ben Starav (1078m)
222. Beinn a'Chreachain (1081m)
223. Beinn a'Chaorainn (1082m)
224. Schiehallion (1083m)
225. Sgurr a'Choire Ghlais (1083m)
226. Beinn Dearg (1084m)
227. Beinn a'Chlachair (1087m)
228. Bynack More (1090m)
229. Stob Ghabhar (1090m)
230. Sgurr nan Clach Geala (1093m)
231. Sgurr Choinnich Mor (1094m)
232. Sgurr a'Mhaim (1099m)
233. Creise (1100m)
234. Beinn Eibhinn (1102m)
235. Mullach Fraoch-choire (1102m)
236. Beinn Ghlas (1103m)
237. Stob a'Choire Mheadhoin (1106m)
238. Meall a'Bhuiridh (1108m)
239. Sgurr nan Conbhairean (1109m)
240. Carn a'Choire Bhoidheach (1110m)
241. Sgurr Mor (1112m)
242. Tom a'Choinich (1113m)
243. Monadh Mor (1115m)
244. Stob Coire an Laoigh (1116m)
245. Stob Coire Easain (1116m)
246. An Stuc (1118m)
247. Meall Garbh (1118m)
248. Sgor Gaoith (1118m)
249. Aonach Beag (1118m)
250. A'Chraileag (1120m)
251. Ben Cruachan (1126m)
252. Beinn a'Ghlo - Carn nan Gabhar (1129m)
253. Creag Meagaidh (1129m)
254. Ben Lui (1130m)
255. Binnein Mor (1130m)
256. An Riabhachan (1130m)
257. Geal-charn (1132m)
258. Ben Alder (1148m)
259. Bidean nam Bian (1150m)
260. Sgurr na Lapaich (1150m)
261. Sgurr nan Ceathreamhnan (1151m)
262. Derry Cairngorm (1155m)
263. Lochnagar - Cac Carn Beag (1155m)
264. Beinn Bhrotain (1157m)
265. Stob Binnein (1165m)
266. Ben Avon - Leabaidh an Daimh Bhuidhe (1171m)
267. Ben More (1174m)
268. Stob Choire Claurigh (1177m)
269. Mam Sodhail (1181m)
270. Beinn Mheadhoin (1182m)
271. Carn Eige [Carn Eighe] (1183m)
272. Beinn a'Bhuird [Beinn a'Bhuird North Top] (1197m)
273. Ben Lawers (1214m)
274. Carn Mor Dearg (1220m)
275. Aonach Mor (1221m)
276. Aonach Beag (1234m)
277. Cairn Gorm (1245m)
278. Sgor an Lochain Uaine (1258m)
279. Cairn Toul (1291m)
280. Braeriach (1296m)
281. Ben Macdui (1309m)
282. Ben Nevis (1344m)

Copyright © 2021 John Backpackers Publishing

1 hr 9

Ben Vane
Height: 915m
Grid Ref: NN 27757 09837

CAIRNDOW
G83 7BF

Date: ----------------------------------
Ascent Start Time: --------------------
Descent Start Time: -------------------
Peak Time: -----------------------------
Finish Time: ---------------------------
Ascent Duration: -----------------------
Descent Duration: ---------------------
Total Time: ----------------------------
Total Distance Covered: ---------------
Weather Conditions:
Temperature: --------- ○ ○ ○ ○ ○ ○
Wind: -----------

(poor) (great)
Difficulty: ○ ○ ○ ○ ○ ○ ○ ○ ○ ○
Fufillment: ○ ○ ○ ○ ○ ○ ○ ○ ○ ○
Scenery: ○ ○ ○ ○ ○ ○ ○ ○ ○ ○
Companions: -----------------

Notes/Photos:

Garve?
IV23 2QT

Beinn Teallach
Height: 915m
Grid Ref: NN 36139 85964

ROYBRIDGE
LOCHABER

Date: ----------------------------------
Ascent Start Time: ---------------------
Descent Start Time: --------------------
Peak Time: -----------------------------
Finish Time: ---------------------------
Ascent Duration: -----------------------
Descent Duration: ----------------------
Total Time: ----------------------------
Total Distance Covered: ----------------
Weather Conditions:
Temperature: --------- ○ ○ ○ ○ ○ ○
Wind: -----------

(poor) (great)
Difficulty: ○ ○ ○ ○ ○ ○ ○ ○ ○ ○
Fufillment: ○ ○ ○ ○ ○ ○ ○ ○ ○ ○
Scenery: ○ ○ ○ ○ ○ ○ ○ ○ ○ ○
Companions: -----------------

Notes/Photos:

CRAINLARICH
FK20 8SB

Beinn a' Chleibh

Height: 916m
Grid Ref: NN 25058 25598

Date: ---

Ascent Start Time: ---

Descent Start Time: ---

Peak Time: ---

Finish Time: ---

Ascent Duration: ---

Descent Duration: ---

Total Time: ---

Total Distance Covered: ---

Weather Conditions:

Temperature: ---

Wind: ---

(poor) (great)
Difficulty: ○ ○ ○ ○ ○ ○ ○ ○ ○
Fufillment: ○ ○ ○ ○ ○ ○ ○ ○ ○
Scenery: ○ ○ ○ ○ ○ ○ ○ ○ ○
Companions: ---

Notes/Photos:

Geal-Charn

WEST OF DRUMOCHTER (A9)

Height: 917m
Grid Ref: NN 59646 78252

Date: ----
Ascent Start Time: ----
Descent Start Time: ----
Peak Time: ----
Finish Time: ----
Ascent Duration: ----
Descent Duration: ----
Total Time: ----
Total Distance Covered: ----
Weather Conditions: ☼ ⛅ ☁ 🌧 🌬 ❄
Temperature: ---- ○ ○ ○ ○ ○ ○
Wind: ----

Difficulty: (poor) ○○○○○○○○○ (great)
Fufillment: ○○○○○○○○○
Scenery: ○○○○○○○○○
Companions: ----

Notes/Photos:

BALLATER

Càrn Aosda

Height: 917m
Grid Ref: NO 13398 79155

Date: ----------------------------

Ascent Start Time: --------------------

Descent Start Time: -------------------

Peak Time: --------------------------

Finish Time: -------------------------

Ascent Duration: ----------------------

Descent Duration: ---------------------

Total Time: -------------------------

Total Distance Covered: --------------

Weather Conditions:

Temperature: ---------- ○ ○ ○ ○ ○ ○

Wind: -----------

(poor) (great)
Difficulty: ○ ○ ○ ○ ○ ○ ○ ○ ○

Fufillment: ○ ○ ○ ○ ○ ○ ○ ○ ○

Scenery: ○ ○ ○ ○ ○ ○ ○ ○ ○

Companions: -----------------

Notes/Photos:

ISLE OF SKYE

Sgùrr a' Mhadaidh
Height: 918m
Grid Ref: NG 44705 23500

Date: ----------------------------------

Ascent Start Time: ---------------------

Descent Start Time: --------------------

Peak Time: -----------------------------

Finish Time: ---------------------------

Ascent Duration: -----------------------

Descent Duration: ----------------------

Total Time: ----------------------------

Total Distance Covered: ----------------

Weather Conditions:

Temperature: ---------

Wind: ----------

(poor) (great)
Difficulty: ○ ○ ○ ○ ○ ○ ○ ○ ○

Fufillment: ○ ○ ○ ○ ○ ○ ○ ○ ○

Scenery: ○ ○ ○ ○ ○ ○ ○ ○ ○

Companions: ---------------

Notes/Photos:

Ruadh Stac Mor

ACHNASHEEN
IV22 2HH

Height: 918m
Grid Ref: NH 01856 75643

Date: ----------------------------------
Ascent Start Time: --------------------
Descent Start Time: -------------------
Peak Time: ------------------------------
Finish Time: ----------------------------
Ascent Duration: ------------------------
Descent Duration: -----------------------
Total Time: -----------------------------
Total Distance Covered: -----------------
Weather Conditions:
Temperature: ---------
Wind: -----------

(poor) (great)
Difficulty: ○ ○ ○ ○ ○ ○ ○ ○ ○ ○
Fufillment: ○ ○ ○ ○ ○ ○ ○ ○ ○ ○
Scenery: ○ ○ ○ ○ ○ ○ ○ ○ ○ ○
Companions: -----------------

Notes/Photos:

Meall na Teanga FORT WILLIAM (LOCH LOCHY)

Height: 918m
Grid Ref: NN 22026 92461

Date: ----------------------------------

Ascent Start Time: --------------------

Descent Start Time: -------------------

Peak Time: -----------------------------

Finish Time: ---------------------------

Ascent Duration: -----------------------

Descent Duration: ----------------------

Total Time: -----------------------------

Total Distance Covered: ---------------

Weather Conditions: ☀ ⛅ ☁ 🌧 ⛈ ❄

Temperature: -------- ○ ○ ○ ○ ○ ○

Wind: -----------

(poor)   (great)
Difficulty: ○ ○ ○ ○ ○ ○ ○ ○ ○ ○

Fufillment: ○ ○ ○ ○ ○ ○ ○ ○ ○ ○

Scenery: ○ ○ ○ ○ ○ ○ ○ ○ ○ ○

Companions: ----------------

Notes/Photos:

3-27

Creag nan Damh
Height: 918m
Grid Ref: NG 98352 11191

PH35 Kyle 4HD

Date: ....
Ascent Start Time: ....
Descent Start Time: ....
Peak Time: ....
Finish Time: ....
Ascent Duration: ....
Descent Duration: ....
Total Time: ....
Total Distance Covered: ....
Weather Conditions:
Temperature: ....
Wind: ....

(poor) (great)
Difficulty: ○ ○ ○ ○ ○ ○ ○ ○ ○ ○
Fufillment: ○ ○ ○ ○ ○ ○ ○ ○ ○ ○
Scenery: ○ ○ ○ ○ ○ ○ ○ ○ ○ ○
Companions: ....
....
....
....

Notes/Photos:

3.48

A'Ghlas-Bheinn
Height: 918m
Grid Ref: NH 00825 23093

Kyle
IV40 8HD

Date: ----------------------------------
Ascent Start Time: --------------------
Descent Start Time: -------------------
Peak Time: ----------------------------
Finish Time: --------------------------
Ascent Duration: ----------------------
Descent Duration: ---------------------
Total Time: ---------------------------
Total Distance Covered: ---------------
Weather Conditions: ☀ ⛅ ☁ 🌧 ⛈ ❄
Temperature: --------- ○ ○ ○ ○ ○ ○
Wind: -----------

(poor)   (great)
Difficulty: ○ ○ ○ ○ ○ ○ ○ ○ ○
Fufillment: ○ ○ ○ ○ ○ ○ ○ ○ ○
Scenery: ○ ○ ○ ○ ○ ○ ○ ○ ○
Companions: -----------------

Notes/Photos:

3.25

Gairich
Height: 919m
Grid Ref: NN 02593 99570

Invergarry
PH34 4EL

Date: ....
Ascent Start Time: ....
Descent Start Time: ....
Peak Time: ....
Finish Time: ....
Ascent Duration: ....
Descent Duration: ....
Total Time: ....
Total Distance Covered: ....
Weather Conditions:
Temperature: ....
Wind: ....

(poor) (great)
Difficulty: ○ ○ ○ ○ ○ ○ ○ ○ ○
Fufillment: ○ ○ ○ ○ ○ ○ ○ ○ ○
Scenery: ○ ○ ○ ○ ○ ○ ○ ○ ○
Companions: ....
....
....
....

Notes/Photos:

Carn Sgulain
Height: 920m
Grid Ref: NH 68304 05811

Date: ------------------------------

Ascent Start Time: --------------------

Descent Start Time: -------------------

Peak Time: ---------------------------

Finish Time: --------------------------

Ascent Duration: ----------------------

Descent Duration: ---------------------

Total Time: --------------------------

Total Distance Covered: --------------

Weather Conditions:

Temperature: ---------

Wind: ----------

(poor) (great)
Difficulty: ○ ○ ○ ○ ○ ○ ○ ○ ○ ○

Fufillment: ○ ○ ○ ○ ○ ○ ○ ○ ○ ○

Scenery: ○ ○ ○ ○ ○ ○ ○ ○ ○ ○

Companions: ---------------

Notes/Photos:

Sgiath Chùil

Height: 921m
Grid Ref: NN 46293 31785

Date: ----------------------------------

Ascent Start Time: --------------------

Descent Start Time: -------------------

Peak Time: ----------------------------

Finish Time: --------------------------

Ascent Duration: ----------------------

Descent Duration: ---------------------

Total Time: ---------------------------

Total Distance Covered: ---------------

Weather Conditions:

Temperature: ---------

Wind: ----------

(poor) (great)
Difficulty: ○ ○ ○ ○ ○ ○ ○ ○ ○

Fufillment: ○ ○ ○ ○ ○ ○ ○ ○ ○

Scenery: ○ ○ ○ ○ ○ ○ ○ ○ ○

Companions: ----------------

Notes/Photos:

An Socach

Height: 921m
Grid Ref: NO 07939 80007

Date: ----------------------------------
Ascent Start Time: --------------------
Descent Start Time: -------------------
Peak Time: ----------------------------
Finish Time: --------------------------
Ascent Duration: ----------------------
Descent Duration: ---------------------
Total Time: ---------------------------
Total Distance Covered: ---------------
Weather Conditions: ☼ ⛅ ☁ 🌧 🌬 ❄
Temperature: -------- ○ ○ ○ ○ ○ ○
Wind: ----------

Difficulty: (poor) ○ ○ ○ ○ ○ ○ ○ ○ ○ ○ (great)
Fufillment: ○ ○ ○ ○ ○ ○ ○ ○ ○ ○
Scenery: ○ ○ ○ ○ ○ ○ ○ ○ ○ ○
Companions: ----------------

Notes/Photos:

Tom na Gruagaich
Height: 922m
Grid Ref: NG 85961 60141

Date: ------------------------------
Ascent Start Time: ------------------
Descent Start Time: -----------------
Peak Time: --------------------------
Finish Time: ------------------------
Ascent Duration: --------------------
Descent Duration: -------------------
Total Time: -------------------------
Total Distance Covered: -------------
Weather Conditions:
Temperature: ---------
Wind: ----------

(poor) (great)
Difficulty: ○ ○ ○ ○ ○ ○ ○ ○ ○
Fufillment: ○ ○ ○ ○ ○ ○ ○ ○ ○
Scenery: ○ ○ ○ ○ ○ ○ ○ ○ ○
Companions: -------------------

○ ○ ○ ○ ○ ○

Notes/Photos:

Sgùrr nan Each

Height: 923m
Grid Ref: NH 18467 69757

Date: ------------------------------------
Ascent Start Time: ---------------------
Descent Start Time: --------------------
Peak Time: ----------------------------
Finish Time: --------------------------
Ascent Duration: ----------------------
Descent Duration: ---------------------
Total Time: ---------------------------
Total Distance Covered: ---------------
Weather Conditions: ☀ ⛅ ☁ 🌧 🌦 ❄
Temperature: --------- ○ ○ ○ ○ ○ ○
Wind: -----------

(poor) (great)
Difficulty: ○ ○ ○ ○ ○ ○ ○ ○ ○ ○
Fufillment: ○ ○ ○ ○ ○ ○ ○ ○ ○ ○
Scenery: ○ ○ ○ ○ ○ ○ ○ ○ ○ ○
Companions: -----------------

Notes/Photos:

An Coileachan

Height: 923m
Grid Ref: NH 24174 68012

Date: ----------------------------------

Ascent Start Time: --------------------

Descent Start Time: -------------------

Peak Time: ------------------------------

Finish Time: ---------------------------

Ascent Duration: ----------------------

Descent Duration: ---------------------

Total Time: -----------------------------

Total Distance Covered: --------------

Weather Conditions: ☀ ⛅ ☁ 🌧 ⛈ ❄

Temperature: ---------- ○ ○ ○ ○ ○ ○

Wind: -----------

(poor) (great)
Difficulty: ○ ○ ○ ○ ○ ○ ○ ○ ○

Fufillment: ○ ○ ○ ○ ○ ○ ○ ○ ○

Scenery: ○ ○ ○ ○ ○ ○ ○ ○ ○

Companions: ------------------

Notes/Photos:

Sgùrr nan Eag
Height: 924m
Grid Ref: NG 45710 19524

Date: ----------------------------------

Ascent Start Time: ---------------------

Descent Start Time: --------------------

Peak Time: -----------------------------

Finish Time: ---------------------------

Ascent Duration: -----------------------

Descent Duration: ----------------------

Total Time: ----------------------------

Total Distance Covered: ---------------

Weather Conditions: ☀ ⛅ ☁ 🌧 🌦 ❄

Temperature: _____ ○ ○ ○ ○ ○ ○

Wind: ----------

(poor) (great)
Difficulty: ○ ○ ○ ○ ○ ○ ○ ○ ○ ○

Fufillment: ○ ○ ○ ○ ○ ○ ○ ○ ○ ○

Scenery: ○ ○ ○ ○ ○ ○ ○ ○ ○ ○

Companions: ----------------

Notes/Photos:

Creag Pitridh
Height: 924m
Grid Ref: NN 48754 81450

Date: ----------------------------------

Ascent Start Time: --------------------

Descent Start Time: -------------------

Peak Time: -----------------------------

Finish Time: ---------------------------

Ascent Duration: -----------------------

Descent Duration: ----------------------

Total Time: ----------------------------

Total Distance Covered: ---------------

Weather Conditions:

Temperature: ---------

Wind: -----------

(poor) (great)
Difficulty: ○ ○ ○ ○ ○ ○ ○ ○ ○ ○

Fufillment: ○ ○ ○ ○ ○ ○ ○ ○ ○ ○

Scenery: ○ ○ ○ ○ ○ ○ ○ ○ ○ ○

Companions: ----------------

Notes/Photos:

Stob Coire Raineach

Height: 925m
Grid Ref: NN 19144 54787

Date: ----------------------------------
Ascent Start Time: ---------------------
Descent Start Time: --------------------
Peak Time: -----------------------------
Finish Time: ---------------------------
Ascent Duration: -----------------------
Descent Duration: ----------------------
Total Time: ----------------------------
Total Distance Covered: ----------------
Weather Conditions: ☼ ⛅ ☁ 🌧 🌦 ❄
Temperature: --------- ○ ○ ○ ○ ○ ○
Wind: -----------

(poor) Difficulty: ○ ○ ○ ○ ○ ○ ○ ○ ○ ○ (great)
Fulfillment: ○ ○ ○ ○ ○ ○ ○ ○ ○ ○
Scenery: ○ ○ ○ ○ ○ ○ ○ ○ ○ ○
Companions: ----------------

Notes/Photos:

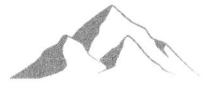

Seana Bhraigh
Height: 926m
Grid Ref: NH 28183 87872

Date: ----------------------------------

Ascent Start Time: --------------------

Descent Start Time: -------------------

Peak Time: -----------------------------

Finish Time: ----------------------------

Ascent Duration: -----------------------

Descent Duration: ----------------------

Total Time: -----------------------------

Total Distance Covered: ---------------

Weather Conditions:

Temperature: ---------- ○ ○ ○ ○ ○ ○

Wind: -----------

(poor) (great)
Difficulty: ○ ○ ○ ○ ○ ○ ○ ○ ○

Fufillment: ○ ○ ○ ○ ○ ○ ○ ○ ○

Scenery: ○ ○ ○ ○ ○ ○ ○ ○ ○

Companions: -----------------------

Notes/Photos:

Meall a'Choire Leith

Height: 926m
Grid Ref: NN 61251 43874

Date: ---------------------------------

Ascent Start Time: ---------------------

Descent Start Time: --------------------

Peak Time: ----------------------------

Finish Time: --------------------------

Ascent Duration: ----------------------

Descent Duration: ---------------------

Total Time: ---------------------------

Total Distance Covered: ---------------

Weather Conditions: ☀ ⛅ ☁ 🌧 ⛈ ❄

Temperature: -------- ○ ○ ○ ○ ○ ○

Wind: -----------

(poor) (great)
Difficulty: ○ ○ ○ ○ ○ ○ ○ ○ ○

Fufillment: ○ ○ ○ ○ ○ ○ ○ ○ ○

Scenery: ○ ○ ○ ○ ○ ○ ○ ○ ○

Companions: ----------------

Notes/Photos:

Geal Charn

Height: 926m
Grid Ref: NN 56146 98758

Date: ---------------------------------
Ascent Start Time: --------------------
Descent Start Time: -------------------
Peak Time: ----------------------------
Finish Time: --------------------------
Ascent Duration: ----------------------
Descent Duration: ---------------------
Total Time: ---------------------------
Total Distance Covered: ---------------
Weather Conditions: ☀ ⛅ ☁ 🌧 🌦 ❄
Temperature: --------- ○ ○ ○ ○ ○ ○
Wind: -----------

Difficulty: (poor) ○ ○ ○ ○ ○ ○ ○ ○ ○ (great)
Fufillment: ○ ○ ○ ○ ○ ○ ○ ○ ○
Scenery: ○ ○ ○ ○ ○ ○ ○ ○ ○
Companions: ------------------

Notes/Photos:

Eididh nan Clach Geala

Height: 926m
Grid Ref: NH 25790 84204

Date: ----------------------------------
Ascent Start Time: --------------------
Descent Start Time: -------------------
Peak Time: ----------------------------
Finish Time: --------------------------
Ascent Duration: ----------------------
Descent Duration: ---------------------
Total Time: ---------------------------
Total Distance Covered: ---------------
Weather Conditions: ☀ ⛅ ☁ 🌧 🌦 ❄
Temperature: --------- ○ ○ ○ ○ ○ ○
Wind: -----------

                              (poor)   (great)
Difficulty: ○ ○ ○ ○ ○ ○ ○ ○ ○
Fufillment: ○ ○ ○ ○ ○ ○ ○ ○ ○
Scenery: ○ ○ ○ ○ ○ ○ ○ ○ ○
Companions: ----------------

Notes/Photos:

Beinn Liath Mhor

Height: 926m
Grid Ref: NG 96412 51970

Date: ------------------------------

Ascent Start Time: --------------------

Descent Start Time: ------------------

Peak Time: ---------------------

Finish Time: -------------------------

Ascent Duration: -----------------------

Descent Duration: ----------------------

Total Time: --------------------------

Total Distance Covered: ---------------

Weather Conditions: ☀ ⛅ ☁ 🌧 ⛈ ❄

Temperature: --------- ○ ○ ○ ○ ○ ○

Wind: -----------

(poor) (great)
Difficulty: ○ ○ ○ ○ ○ ○ ○ ○ ○

Fufillment: ○ ○ ○ ○ ○ ○ ○ ○ ○

Scenery: ○ ○ ○ ○ ○ ○ ○ ○ ○

Companions: -----------------

Notes/Photos:

Beinn Narnain

Height: 927m
Grid Ref: NN 27172 06648

Date: ------------------------------

Ascent Start Time: -------------------

Descent Start Time: ------------------

Peak Time: ---------------------------

Finish Time: -------------------------

Ascent Duration: ---------------------

Descent Duration: --------------------

Total Time: --------------------------

Total Distance Covered: --------------

Weather Conditions: ☀ ⛅ ☁ 🌧 🌦 ❄

Temperature: ------- ○ ○ ○ ○ ○ ○

Wind: -----------

(poor) (great)
Difficulty: ○ ○ ○ ○ ○ ○ ○ ○ ○ ○

Fufillment: ○ ○ ○ ○ ○ ○ ○ ○ ○ ○

Scenery: ○ ○ ○ ○ ○ ○ ○ ○ ○ ○

Companions: ----------------

Notes/Photos:

Ben Hope
Height: 927m
Grid Ref: NC 47751 50138

Date: ----------------------------------

Ascent Start Time: --------------------

Descent Start Time: -------------------

Peak Time: ----------------------------

Finish Time: --------------------------

Ascent Duration: ----------------------

Descent Duration: ---------------------

Total Time: ---------------------------

Total Distance Covered: ---------------

Weather Conditions: ☀ ⛅ ☁ 🌧 🌩 ❄

Temperature: --------- ○ ○ ○ ○ ○ ○

Wind: -----------

(poor) (great)
Difficulty: ○ ○ ○ ○ ○ ○ ○ ○ ○

Fufillment: ○ ○ ○ ○ ○ ○ ○ ○ ○

Scenery: ○ ○ ○ ○ ○ ○ ○ ○ ○

Companions: --------------------

Notes/Photos:

Bla Bheinn
Height: 928m
Grid Ref: NG 52995 21731

Date: ----------------------------------

Ascent Start Time: --------------------

Descent Start Time: -------------------

Peak Time: ----------------------------

Finish Time: --------------------------

Ascent Duration: ----------------------

Descent Duration: ---------------------

Total Time: ---------------------------

Total Distance Covered: ---------------

Weather Conditions: ☀ ⛅ ☁ 🌧 🌬 ❄

Temperature: --------- ○ ○ ○ ○ ○ ○

Wind: -----------

(poor) (great)
Difficulty: ○ ○ ○ ○ ○ ○ ○ ○ ○

Fufillment: ○ ○ ○ ○ ○ ○ ○ ○ ○

Scenery: ○ ○ ○ ○ ○ ○ ○ ○ ○

Companions: ----------------

Notes/Photos:

Mayar

Height: 928m
Grid Ref: NO 24083 73740

Date: ---------------------------------
Ascent Start Time: --------------------
Descent Start Time: -------------------
Peak Time: ----------------------------
Finish Time: --------------------------
Ascent Duration: ----------------------
Descent Duration: ---------------------
Total Time: ---------------------------
Total Distance Covered: ---------------
Weather Conditions: ☀ ⛅ ☁ 🌧 🌦 ❄
Temperature: --------- ○ ○ ○ ○ ○ ○
Wind: -----------

                   (poor)   (great)
Difficulty: ○ ○ ○ ○ ○ ○ ○ ○ ○
Fufillment: ○ ○ ○ ○ ○ ○ ○ ○ ○
Scenery: ○ ○ ○ ○ ○ ○ ○ ○ ○
Companions: ---------------

Notes/Photos:

Meall nan Eun

Height: 928m
Grid Ref: NN 19252 44894

Date: ----------------------------------

Ascent Start Time: --------------------

Descent Start Time: -------------------

Peak Time: ----------------------------

Finish Time: --------------------------

Ascent Duration: ----------------------

Descent Duration: ---------------------

Total Time: ---------------------------

Total Distance Covered: ---------------

Weather Conditions:

Temperature: ---------

Wind: ----------

(poor) (great)
Difficulty: ○ ○ ○ ○ ○ ○ ○ ○ ○

Fufillment: ○ ○ ○ ○ ○ ○ ○ ○ ○

Scenery: ○ ○ ○ ○ ○ ○ ○ ○ ○

Companions: ----------------

Notes/Photos:

Moruisg
Height: 928m
Grid Ref: NH 10117 49927

Date: ----------------------------------

Ascent Start Time: --------------------

Descent Start Time: ------------------

Peak Time: ----------------------------

Finish Time: --------------------------

Ascent Duration: ---------------------

Descent Duration: --------------------

Total Time: ---------------------------

Total Distance Covered: -------------

Weather Conditions: ☀ ⛅ ☁ 🌧 ⛈ ❄

Temperature: --------- ○ ○ ○ ○ ○ ○

Wind: -----------

Difficulty: (poor) ○ ○ ○ ○ ○ ○ ○ ○ ○ (great)

Fufillment: ○ ○ ○ ○ ○ ○ ○ ○ ○

Scenery: ○ ○ ○ ○ ○ ○ ○ ○ ○

Companions: ------------------

Notes/Photos:

A'Chailleach

Height: 930m
Grid Ref: NH 68112 04168

Date:	Difficulty: (poor) ○○○○○○○○○ (great)
Ascent Start Time:	Fufillment: ○○○○○○○○○
Descent Start Time:	Scenery: ○○○○○○○○○
Peak Time:	Companions:
Finish Time:	
Ascent Duration:	
Descent Duration:	
Total Time:	

Total Distance Covered:

Weather Conditions: ☀ ⛅ ☁ 🌧 🌬 ❄

Temperature: ○ ○ ○ ○ ○ ○

Wind:

Notes/Photos:

Beinn Bhreac

Height: 931m
Grid Ref: NN 32155 00064

Date: ....

Ascent Start Time: ....

Descent Start Time: ....

Peak Time: ....

Finish Time: ....

Ascent Duration: ....

Descent Duration: ....

Total Time: ....

Total Distance Covered: ....

Weather Conditions: ☼ ⛅ ☁ 🌧 ⛈ ❄

Temperature: .... ○ ○ ○ ○ ○ ○

Wind: ....

          (poor)   (great)
Difficulty: ○ ○ ○ ○ ○ ○ ○ ○ ○

Fufillment: ○ ○ ○ ○ ○ ○ ○ ○ ○

Scenery: ○ ○ ○ ○ ○ ○ ○ ○ ○

Companions: ....

Notes/Photos:

Ben Chonzie

Height: 931m
Grid Ref: NN 77326 30850

Date: ....
Ascent Start Time: ....
Descent Start Time: ....
Peak Time: ....
Finish Time: ....
Ascent Duration: ....
Descent Duration: ....
Total Time: ....
Total Distance Covered: ....
Weather Conditions: ☀ ⛅ ☁ 🌧 ⛈ ❄
Temperature: .... ○ ○ ○ ○ ○ ○
Wind: ....

Difficulty: (poor) ○ ○ ○ ○ ○ ○ ○ ○ ○ (great)
Fufillment: ○ ○ ○ ○ ○ ○ ○ ○ ○
Scenery: ○ ○ ○ ○ ○ ○ ○ ○ ○
Companions: ....
....
....
....

Notes/Photos:

Meall Buidhe

Height: 932m
Grid Ref: NN 49841 49937

Date: ----------------------------------
Ascent Start Time: ----------------------
Descent Start Time: --------------------
Peak Time: ----------------------------
Finish Time: --------------------------
Ascent Duration: ----------------------
Descent Duration: --------------------
Total Time: --------------------------
Total Distance Covered: --------------
Weather Conditions: ☀ ⛅ ☁ 🌧 🌦 ❄
Temperature: --------- ○ ○ ○ ○ ○ ○
Wind: -----------

(poor) (great)
Difficulty: ○ ○ ○ ○ ○ ○ ○ ○ ○ ○
Fufillment: ○ ○ ○ ○ ○ ○ ○ ○ ○ ○
Scenery: ○ ○ ○ ○ ○ ○ ○ ○ ○ ○
Companions: -----------------

Notes/Photos:

Beinn Chabhair

Height: 933m
Grid Ref: NN 36763 17950

Date: ....

Ascent Start Time: ....

Descent Start Time: ....

Peak Time: ....

Finish Time: ....

Ascent Duration: ....

Descent Duration: ....

Total Time: ....

Total Distance Covered: ....

Weather Conditions: ☀ ⛅ ☁ 🌧 🌦 ❄

Temperature: .... ○ ○ ○ ○ ○ ○

Wind: ....

(poor) (great)
Difficulty: ○ ○ ○ ○ ○ ○ ○ ○ ○ ○

Fufillment: ○ ○ ○ ○ ○ ○ ○ ○ ○ ○

Scenery: ○ ○ ○ ○ ○ ○ ○ ○ ○ ○

Companions: ....

....

....

....

Notes/Photos:

Fionn Bheinn

Height: 933m
Grid Ref: NH 14752 62137

Date: ----------------------------------
Ascent Start Time: ---------------------
Descent Start Time: --------------------
Peak Time: -----------------------------
Finish Time: ---------------------------
Ascent Duration: -----------------------
Descent Duration: ----------------------
Total Time: ----------------------------
Total Distance Covered: ---------------
Weather Conditions:
Temperature: --------- ○ ○ ○ ○ ○ ○
Wind: ----------

(poor) (great)
Difficulty: ○ ○ ○ ○ ○ ○ ○ ○ ○ ○
Fufillment: ○ ○ ○ ○ ○ ○ ○ ○ ○ ○
Scenery: ○ ○ ○ ○ ○ ○ ○ ○ ○ ○
Companions: ---------------

Notes/Photos:

Maol Chean-dearg

Height: 933m
Grid Ref: NG 92409 49899

Date: ---------------------------------

Ascent Start Time: ---------------------

Descent Start Time: -------------------

Peak Time: ---------------------------

Finish Time: -------------------------

Ascent Duration: ---------------------

Descent Duration: --------------------

Total Time: --------------------------

Total Distance Covered: ---------------

Weather Conditions: ☼ ⛅ ☁ 🌧 🌬 ❄

Temperature: --------- ○ ○ ○ ○ ○ ○

Wind: -----------

(poor) (great)
Difficulty: ○ ○ ○ ○ ○ ○ ○ ○ ○ ○

Fufillment: ○ ○ ○ ○ ○ ○ ○ ○ ○ ○

Scenery: ○ ○ ○ ○ ○ ○ ○ ○ ○ ○

Companions: ------------------

Notes/Photos:

The Cairnwell

Height: 933m
Grid Ref: NO 13487 77352

Date: ----------------------------------

Ascent Start Time: --------------------

Descent Start Time: -------------------

Peak Time: ---------------------------

Finish Time: --------------------------

Ascent Duration: ----------------------

Descent Duration: ---------------------

Total Time: ---------------------------

Total Distance Covered: --------------

Weather Conditions: ☀️ ⛅ ☁️ 🌧️ ⛈️ ❄️

Temperature: ---------- ○ ○ ○ ○ ○ ○

Wind: -----------

(poor) (great)
Difficulty: ○ ○ ○ ○ ○ ○ ○ ○ ○

Fufillment: ○ ○ ○ ○ ○ ○ ○ ○ ○

Scenery: ○ ○ ○ ○ ○ ○ ○ ○ ○

Companions: --------------------

Notes/Photos:

Am Basteir

Height: 934m
Grid Ref: NG 46569 25290

Date: ----------------------------------

Ascent Start Time: --------------------

Descent Start Time: -------------------

Peak Time: ----------------------------

Finish Time: --------------------------

Ascent Duration: ----------------------

Descent Duration: ---------------------

Total Time: ---------------------------

Total Distance Covered: ---------------

Weather Conditions:

Temperature: ---------

Wind: ----------

(poor) (great)
Difficulty: ○ ○ ○ ○ ○ ○ ○ ○ ○ ○

Fufillment: ○ ○ ○ ○ ○ ○ ○ ○ ○ ○

Scenery: ○ ○ ○ ○ ○ ○ ○ ○ ○ ○

Companions: ----------------

Notes/Photos:

Meall a'Chrasgaidh

Height: 934m
Grid Ref: NH 18484 73308

Date: ----------------------------------

Ascent Start Time: --------------------

Descent Start Time: -------------------

Peak Time: ----------------------------

Finish Time: --------------------------

Ascent Duration: ----------------------

Descent Duration: ---------------------

Total Time: ---------------------------

Total Distance Covered: --------------

Weather Conditions: ☀ ⛅ ☁ 🌧 🌦 ❄

Temperature: --------- ○ ○ ○ ○ ○ ○

Wind: ----------

(poor) (great)
Difficulty: ○ ○ ○ ○ ○ ○ ○ ○ ○

Fufillment: ○ ○ ○ ○ ○ ○ ○ ○ ○

Scenery: ○ ○ ○ ○ ○ ○ ○ ○ ○

Companions: --------------------

Notes/Photos:

Beinn na Lap
Height: 936m
Grid Ref: NN 37619 69576

Date: ------------------------------

Ascent Start Time: --------------------

Descent Start Time: ------------------

Peak Time: --------------------------

Finish Time: -------------------------

Ascent Duration: ---------------------

Descent Duration: --------------------

Total Time: --------------------------

Total Distance Covered: --------------

Weather Conditions: ☀️ ⛅ ☁️ 🌧️ 🌦️ ❄️

Temperature: --------- ○ ○ ○ ○ ○ ○

Wind: -----------

(poor) Difficulty: ○ ○ ○ ○ ○ ○ ○ ○ ○ (great)

Fufillment: ○ ○ ○ ○ ○ ○ ○ ○ ○

Scenery: ○ ○ ○ ○ ○ ○ ○ ○ ○

Companions: ---------------

Notes/Photos:

Beinn Sgulaird
Height: 937m
Grid Ref: NN 05307 46079

Date: ----------------------------

Ascent Start Time: -------------------

Descent Start Time: -----------------

Peak Time: ---------------------

Finish Time: -------------------------

Ascent Duration: ----------------------

Descent Duration: ---------------------

Total Time: ----------------------

Total Distance Covered: ---------------

Weather Conditions:

Temperature: ---------

Wind: ----------

(poor) (great)
Difficulty: ○ ○ ○ ○ ○ ○ ○ ○ ○ ○

Fufillment: ○ ○ ○ ○ ○ ○ ○ ○ ○ ○

Scenery: ○ ○ ○ ○ ○ ○ ○ ○ ○ ○

Companions: ----------------

Notes/Photos:

Beinn Tarsuinn

Height: 937m
Grid Ref: NH 03963 72782

Date: ....

Ascent Start Time: ....

Descent Start Time: ....

Peak Time: ....

Finish Time: ....

Ascent Duration: ....

Descent Duration: ....

Total Time: ....

Total Distance Covered: ....

Weather Conditions: ☀ ⛅ ☁ 🌧 🌦 ❄

Temperature: .... ○ ○ ○ ○ ○ ○

Wind: ....

(poor) (great)
Difficulty: ○ ○ ○ ○ ○ ○ ○ ○ ○ ○

Fufillment: ○ ○ ○ ○ ○ ○ ○ ○ ○ ○

Scenery: ○ ○ ○ ○ ○ ○ ○ ○ ○ ○

Companions: ....

....

....

....

Notes/Photos:

Sron a'Choire Ghairbh

Height: 937m
Grid Ref: NN 22250 94550

Date: ----------------------------------

Ascent Start Time: --------------------

Descent Start Time: -------------------

Peak Time: ----------------------------

Finish Time: --------------------------

Ascent Duration: ----------------------

Descent Duration: ---------------------

Total Time: ---------------------------

Total Distance Covered: ---------------

Weather Conditions: ☀ ⛅ ☁ 🌧 ⛈ ❄

Temperature: --------- ○ ○ ○ ○ ○ ○

Wind: -----------

(poor) (great)
Difficulty: ○ ○ ○ ○ ○ ○ ○ ○ ○

Fufillment: ○ ○ ○ ○ ○ ○ ○ ○ ○

Scenery: ○ ○ ○ ○ ○ ○ ○ ○ ○

Companions: ---------------

Notes/Photos:

A'Bhuidheanach Bheag

Height: 937m
Grid Ref: NN 66061 77585

Date: ....

Ascent Start Time: ....

Descent Start Time: ....

Peak Time: ....

Finish Time: ....

Ascent Duration: ....

Descent Duration: ....

Total Time: ....

Total Distance Covered: ....

Weather Conditions: ☀ ⛅ ☁ 🌧 🌦 ❄

Temperature: .... ○ ○ ○ ○ ○ ○

Wind: ....

(poor) (great)
Difficulty: ○ ○ ○ ○ ○ ○ ○ ○ ○ ○

Fufillment: ○ ○ ○ ○ ○ ○ ○ ○ ○ ○

Scenery: ○ ○ ○ ○ ○ ○ ○ ○ ○ ○

Companions: ....

....

....

....

Notes/Photos:

Luinne Bheinn

Height: 939m
Grid Ref: NG 86983 00729

Date: ....
Ascent Start Time: ....
Descent Start Time: ....
Peak Time: ....
Finish Time: ....
Ascent Duration: ....
Descent Duration: ....
Total Time: ....
Total Distance Covered: ....
Weather Conditions: ☀ ⛅ ☁ 🌧 ⛈ ❄
Temperature: .... ○ ○ ○ ○ ○ ○
Wind: ....

(poor) (great)
Difficulty: ○ ○ ○ ○ ○ ○ ○ ○ ○
Fufillment: ○ ○ ○ ○ ○ ○ ○ ○ ○
Scenery: ○ ○ ○ ○ ○ ○ ○ ○ ○
Companions: ....
....
....
....

Notes/Photos:

Mount Keen

Height: 939m
Grid Ref: NO 40905 86918

Date: ---------------------------------

Ascent Start Time: --------------------

Descent Start Time: -------------------

Peak Time: ----------------------------

Finish Time: --------------------------

Ascent Duration: ----------------------

Descent Duration: ---------------------

Total Time: ---------------------------

Total Distance Covered: ---------------

Weather Conditions:

Temperature: _____ ○ ○ ○ ○ ○ ○

Wind: _____

(poor) (great)
Difficulty: ○ ○ ○ ○ ○ ○ ○ ○ ○

Fufillment: ○ ○ ○ ○ ○ ○ ○ ○ ○

Scenery: ○ ○ ○ ○ ○ ○ ○ ○ ○

Companions: ------------------

Notes/Photos:

Mullach nan Coirean

Height: 939m
Grid Ref: NN 12237 66234

Date: ----------------------------------

Ascent Start Time: --------------------

Descent Start Time: ------------------

Peak Time: ------------------------------

Finish Time: ----------------------------

Ascent Duration: -----------------------

Descent Duration: ----------------------

Total Time: ------------------------------

Total Distance Covered: ---------------

Weather Conditions:

Temperature: ----------

Wind: -----------

(poor) (great)
Difficulty: ○ ○ ○ ○ ○ ○ ○ ○ ○ ○

Fufillment: ○ ○ ○ ○ ○ ○ ○ ○ ○ ○

Scenery: ○ ○ ○ ○ ○ ○ ○ ○ ○ ○

Companions: --------------------

Notes/Photos:

Beinn a'Chroin

Height: 940m
Grid Ref: NN 38758 18566

Date: ---------------------------------

Ascent Start Time: ---------------------

Descent Start Time: -------------------

Peak Time: ----------------------------

Finish Time: --------------------------

Ascent Duration: ----------------------

Descent Duration: ---------------------

Total Time: ---------------------------

Total Distance Covered: ---------------

Weather Conditions:

Temperature: --------- ○ ○ ○ ○ ○ ○

Wind: -----------

(poor) (great)
Difficulty: ○ ○ ○ ○ ○ ○ ○ ○ ○ ○

Fufillment: ○ ○ ○ ○ ○ ○ ○ ○ ○ ○

Scenery: ○ ○ ○ ○ ○ ○ ○ ○ ○ ○

Companions: ----------------

Notes/Photos:

Carn Dearg
Height: 941m
Grid Ref: NN 41776 66134

Date: ----------------------------------
Ascent Start Time: --------------------
Descent Start Time: -------------------
Peak Time: ----------------------------
Finish Time: --------------------------
Ascent Duration: ----------------------
Descent Duration: ---------------------
Total Time: ---------------------------
Total Distance Covered: ---------------
Weather Conditions: ☀ ⛅ ☁ 🌧 ⛈ ❄
Temperature: --------- ○ ○ ○ ○ ○ ○
Wind: -----------

(poor) (great)
Difficulty: ○ ○ ○ ○ ○ ○ ○ ○ ○
Fufillment: ○ ○ ○ ○ ○ ○ ○ ○ ○
Scenery: ○ ○ ○ ○ ○ ○ ○ ○ ○
Companions: --------------------

Notes/Photos:

Carn na Caim

Height: 941m
Grid Ref: NN 67702 82144

Date: ----------------------------------

Ascent Start Time: ---------------------

Descent Start Time: -------------------

Peak Time: ----------------------------

Finish Time: --------------------------

Ascent Duration: ----------------------

Descent Duration: ---------------------

Total Time: ---------------------------

Total Distance Covered: ---------------

Weather Conditions: ☀ ⛅ ☁ 🌧 ☂ ❄

Temperature: -------- ○ ○ ○ ○ ○ ○

Wind: ----------

                (poor)   (great)
Difficulty: ○ ○ ○ ○ ○ ○ ○ ○ ○ ○

Fufillment: ○ ○ ○ ○ ○ ○ ○ ○ ○ ○

Scenery: ○ ○ ○ ○ ○ ○ ○ ○ ○ ○

Companions: ----------------

Notes/Photos:

1hr 24

Ben Vorlich Crieff FK19 8PZ
Height: 943m
Grid Ref: NN 29513 12467

Ascent Start Time: _____
Descent Start Time: _____
Peak Time: _____
Finish Time: _____
Ascent Duration: _____
Descent Duration: _____
Total Time: _____
Total Distance Covered: _____
Weather Conditions: ☀ ⛅ ☁ 🌧 🌦 ❄
Temperature: _____ ○ ○ ○ ○ ○ ○
Wind: _____

(poor) (great)
Difficulty: ○ ○ ○ ○ ○ ○ ○ ○ ○
Fufillment: ○ ○ ○ ○ ○ ○ ○ ○ ○
Scenery: ○ ○ ○ ○ ○ ○ ○ ○ ○
Companions: _____
_____
_____
_____

Notes/Photos:

Binnein Beag

Height: 943m
Grid Ref: NN 22176 67705

Date: ---------------------------------

Ascent Start Time: --------------------

Descent Start Time: -------------------

Peak Time: ----------------------------

Finish Time: --------------------------

Ascent Duration: ----------------------

Descent Duration: ---------------------

Total Time: ---------------------------

Total Distance Covered: ---------------

Weather Conditions: ☀ ⛅ ☁ 🌧 ⛈ ❄

Temperature: --------- ○ ○ ○ ○ ○ ○

Wind: -----------

(poor) Difficulty: ○ ○ ○ ○ ○ ○ ○ ○ ○ (great)

Fufillment: ○ ○ ○ ○ ○ ○ ○ ○ ○

Scenery: ○ ○ ○ ○ ○ ○ ○ ○ ○

Companions: ------------------

Notes/Photos:

An Socach

Height: 944m
Grid Ref: NO 07939 80007

Date: ---------------------------------

Ascent Start Time: --------------------

Descent Start Time: -------------------

Peak Time: ---------------------------

Finish Time: -------------------------

Ascent Duration: ----------------------

Descent Duration: ---------------------

Total Time: --------------------------

Total Distance Covered: ---------------

Weather Conditions:

Temperature: --------- ○ ○ ○ ○ ○ ○

Wind: ----------

(poor) (great)
Difficulty: ○ ○ ○ ○ ○ ○ ○ ○ ○ ○

Fufillment: ○ ○ ○ ○ ○ ○ ○ ○ ○ ○

Scenery: ○ ○ ○ ○ ○ ○ ○ ○ ○ ○

Companions: ----------------

Notes/Photos:

Sgurr Dubh Mor

Height: 944m
Grid Ref: NG 45763 20535

Date: ------------------------------

Ascent Start Time: --------------------

Descent Start Time: -------------------

Peak Time: ---------------------------

Finish Time: --------------------------

Ascent Duration: ----------------------

Descent Duration: ---------------------

Total Time: ---------------------------

Total Distance Covered: ---------------

Weather Conditions:

Temperature: --------- ○ ○ ○ ○ ○ ○

Wind: -----------

(poor) (great)
Difficulty: ○ ○ ○ ○ ○ ○ ○ ○ ○

Fufillment: ○ ○ ○ ○ ○ ○ ○ ○ ○

Scenery: ○ ○ ○ ○ ○ ○ ○ ○ ○

Companions: ------------------

Notes/Photos:

Sgurr na Sgine

Height: 945m
Grid Ref: NG 94622 11357

Date: ....
Ascent Start Time: ....
Descent Start Time: ....
Peak Time: ....
Finish Time: ....
Ascent Duration: ....
Descent Duration: ....
Total Time: ....
Total Distance Covered: ....
Weather Conditions:
Temperature: ....
Wind: ....

(poor) (great)
Difficulty: ○ ○ ○ ○ ○ ○ ○ ○ ○
Fufillment: ○ ○ ○ ○ ○ ○ ○ ○ ○
Scenery: ○ ○ ○ ○ ○ ○ ○ ○ ○
Companions: ....
....
....
....

Notes/Photos:

Bidein a'Choire Sheasgaich

Height: 945m
Grid Ref: NH 04909 41254

Date: ---
Ascent Start Time: ---
Descent Start Time: ---
Peak Time: ---
Finish Time: ---
Ascent Duration: ---
Descent Duration: ---
Total Time: ---
Total Distance Covered: ---
Weather Conditions:
Temperature: ---
Wind: ---

(poor) (great)
Difficulty: ○ ○ ○ ○ ○ ○ ○ ○ ○
Fufillment: ○ ○ ○ ○ ○ ○ ○ ○ ○
Scenery: ○ ○ ○ ○ ○ ○ ○ ○ ○
Companions: ---

Notes/Photos:

Carn Dearg
Height: 945m
Grid Ref: NH 63570 02388

Date: ....
Ascent Start Time: ....
Descent Start Time: ....
Peak Time: ....
Finish Time: ....
Ascent Duration: ....
Descent Duration: ....
Total Time: ....
Total Distance Covered: ....
Weather Conditions:
Temperature: ....
Wind: ....

(poor) (great)
Difficulty: ○ ○ ○ ○ ○ ○ ○ ○ ○
Fufillment: ○ ○ ○ ○ ○ ○ ○ ○ ○
Scenery: ○ ○ ○ ○ ○ ○ ○ ○ ○
Companions: ....
....
....
....

Notes/Photos:

Stob a'Choire Odhair

Height: 945m
Grid Ref: NN 25735 45973

Date: ----------------------------------

Ascent Start Time: --------------------

Descent Start Time: -------------------

Peak Time: ------------------------------

Finish Time: ----------------------------

Ascent Duration: ------------------------

Descent Duration: -----------------------

Total Time: -----------------------------

Total Distance Covered: ---------------

Weather Conditions:

Temperature: ---------

Wind: -----------

(poor) (great)
Difficulty: ○ ○ ○ ○ ○ ○ ○ ○ ○

Fufillment: ○ ○ ○ ○ ○ ○ ○ ○ ○

Scenery: ○ ○ ○ ○ ○ ○ ○ ○ ○

Companions: ------------------

Notes/Photos:

Beinn Tulaichean
Height: 946m
Grid Ref: NN 41663 19596

Date: ----------------------------------

Ascent Start Time: --------------------

Descent Start Time: -------------------

Peak Time: ----------------------------

Finish Time: --------------------------

Ascent Duration: ----------------------

Descent Duration: ---------------------

Total Time: ---------------------------

Total Distance Covered: ---------------

Weather Conditions:

Temperature: ---------

Wind: ----------

(poor) (great)
Difficulty: ○ ○ ○ ○ ○ ○ ○ ○ ○ ○

Fufillment: ○ ○ ○ ○ ○ ○ ○ ○ ○ ○

Scenery: ○ ○ ○ ○ ○ ○ ○ ○ ○ ○

Companions: -------------------

Notes/Photos:

Carn Bhac

Height: 946m
Grid Ref: NO 05105 83216

Date: ---------------------------------

Ascent Start Time: --------------------

Descent Start Time: -------------------

Peak Time: ----------------------------

Finish Time: --------------------------

Ascent Duration: ----------------------

Descent Duration: ---------------------

Total Time: ---------------------------

Total Distance Covered: ---------------

Weather Conditions:

Temperature: ---------

Wind: ----------

(poor) (great)
Difficulty: ○ ○ ○ ○ ○ ○ ○ ○ ○ ○

Fufillment: ○ ○ ○ ○ ○ ○ ○ ○ ○ ○

Scenery: ○ ○ ○ ○ ○ ○ ○ ○ ○ ○

Companions: ----------------

Notes/Photos:

Meall Buidhe

Height: 946m
Grid Ref: NM 84902 98966

Date: _____

Ascent Start Time: _____

Descent Start Time: _____

Peak Time: _____

Finish Time: _____

Ascent Duration: _____

Descent Duration: _____

Total Time: _____

Total Distance Covered: _____

Weather Conditions: ☀ ⛅ ☁ 🌧 ⛈ ❄

Temperature: _____ ○ ○ ○ ○ ○ ○

Wind: _____

(poor) (great)
Difficulty: ○ ○ ○ ○ ○ ○ ○ ○ ○

Fufillment: ○ ○ ○ ○ ○ ○ ○ ○ ○

Scenery: ○ ○ ○ ○ ○ ○ ○ ○ ○

Companions: _____

_____

_____

_____

Notes/Photos:

Creag a'Mhaim

Height: 947m
Grid Ref: NH 08793 07762

Date: ----------------------------------
Ascent Start Time: ---------------------
Descent Start Time: --------------------
Peak Time: -----------------------------
Finish Time: ---------------------------
Ascent Duration: -----------------------
Descent Duration: ----------------------
Total Time: ----------------------------
Total Distance Covered: ----------------
Weather Conditions: ☀ ⛅ ☁ 🌧 ⛈ ❄
Temperature: --------- ○ ○ ○ ○ ○ ○
Wind: -----------

(poor) (great)
Difficulty: ○ ○ ○ ○ ○ ○ ○ ○ ○
Fufillment: ○ ○ ○ ○ ○ ○ ○ ○ ○
Scenery: ○ ○ ○ ○ ○ ○ ○ ○ ○
Companions: --------------------

Notes/Photos:

Driesh

Height: 947m
Grid Ref: NO 27116 73582

Date: ....
Ascent Start Time: ....
Descent Start Time: ....
Peak Time: ....
Finish Time: ....
Ascent Duration: ....
Descent Duration: ....
Total Time: ....
Total Distance Covered: ....
Weather Conditions: ☀️ ⛅ ☁️ 🌧️ 🌦️ ❄️
Temperature: .... ○ ○ ○ ○ ○ ○
Wind: ....

(poor) (great)
Difficulty: ○ ○ ○ ○ ○ ○ ○ ○ ○ ○
Fufillment: ○ ○ ○ ○ ○ ○ ○ ○ ○ ○
Scenery: ○ ○ ○ ○ ○ ○ ○ ○ ○ ○
Companions: ....
....
....
....

Notes/Photos:

Beinn Bhuidhe

Height: 948m
Grid Ref: NN 20372 18709

Date: ----------------------------------

Ascent Start Time: --------------------

Descent Start Time: -------------------

Peak Time: ----------------------------

Finish Time: --------------------------

Ascent Duration: ----------------------

Descent Duration: ---------------------

Total Time: ---------------------------

Total Distance Covered: ---------------

Weather Conditions: ☀ ⛅ ☁ 🌧 🌦 ❄

Temperature: --------- ○ ○ ○ ○ ○ ○

Wind: -----------

(poor) (great)
Difficulty: ○ ○ ○ ○ ○ ○ ○ ○ ○ ○

Fufillment: ○ ○ ○ ○ ○ ○ ○ ○ ○ ○

Scenery: ○ ○ ○ ○ ○ ○ ○ ○ ○ ○

Companions: -------------------

Notes/Photos:

Sgurr Mhic Choinnich

Height: 948m
Grid Ref: NG 45025 21031

Date: ---

Ascent Start Time: ---

Descent Start Time: ---

Peak Time: ---

Finish Time: ---

Ascent Duration: ---

Descent Duration: ---

Total Time: ---

Total Distance Covered: ---

Weather Conditions:

Temperature: ---

Wind: ---

Difficulty: (poor) ○ ○ ○ ○ ○ ○ ○ ○ ○ ○ (great)

Fufillment: ○ ○ ○ ○ ○ ○ ○ ○ ○ ○

Scenery: ○ ○ ○ ○ ○ ○ ○ ○ ○ ○

Companions: ---

Notes/Photos:

Meall Gorm

Height: 949m
Grid Ref: NH 22194 69572

Date: ----------------------------------

Ascent Start Time: --------------------

Descent Start Time: -------------------

Peak Time: ---------------------------

Finish Time: --------------------------

Ascent Duration: ---------------------

Descent Duration: --------------------

Total Time: ---------------------------

Total Distance Covered: --------------

Weather Conditions:

Temperature: --------- ○ ○ ○ ○ ○ ○

Wind: ----------

(poor) (great)
Difficulty: ○ ○ ○ ○ ○ ○ ○ ○ ○ ○

Fufillment: ○ ○ ○ ○ ○ ○ ○ ○ ○ ○

Scenery: ○ ○ ○ ○ ○ ○ ○ ○ ○ ○

Companions: ----------------

Notes/Photos:

Meall Chuaich

Height: 951m
Grid Ref: NN 71650 87825

Date: ---------------------------------

Ascent Start Time: ---------------------

Descent Start Time: --------------------

Peak Time: ---------------------------

Finish Time: --------------------------

Ascent Duration: ----------------------

Descent Duration: ---------------------

Total Time: ---------------------------

Total Distance Covered: ---------------

Weather Conditions:

Temperature: ---------

Wind: ----------

(poor) (great)
Difficulty: ○ ○ ○ ○ ○ ○ ○ ○ ○

Fufillment: ○ ○ ○ ○ ○ ○ ○ ○ ○

Scenery: ○ ○ ○ ○ ○ ○ ○ ○ ○

Companions: ------------------

Notes/Photos:

Beinn Mhanach

Height: 953m
Grid Ref: NN 37374 41132

Date: ----------------------------------

Ascent Start Time: ---------------------

Descent Start Time: --------------------

Peak Time: -----------------------------

Finish Time: ---------------------------

Ascent Duration: -----------------------

Descent Duration: ----------------------

Total Time: ----------------------------

Total Distance Covered: ---------------

Weather Conditions:

Temperature: ....

Wind: -----------

(poor) (great)
Difficulty: ○ ○ ○ ○ ○ ○ ○ ○ ○

Fufillment: ○ ○ ○ ○ ○ ○ ○ ○ ○

Scenery: ○ ○ ○ ○ ○ ○ ○ ○ ○

Companions: ----------------

Notes/Photos:

Aonach Eagach - Meall Dearg

Height: 953m
Grid Ref: NN 16128 58354

Date: ----

Ascent Start Time: ----

Descent Start Time: ----

Peak Time: ----

Finish Time: ----

Ascent Duration: ----

Descent Duration: ----

Total Time: ----

Total Distance Covered: ----

Weather Conditions:

Temperature: ----

Wind: ----

(poor) (great)
Difficulty: ○ ○ ○ ○ ○ ○ ○ ○ ○

Fufillment: ○ ○ ○ ○ ○ ○ ○ ○ ○

Scenery: ○ ○ ○ ○ ○ ○ ○ ○ ○

Companions: ----

Notes/Photos:

Sgurr nan Coireachan
Height: 953m
Grid Ref: NM 93312 95817

Date: ....

Ascent Start Time: ....

Descent Start Time: ....

Peak Time: ....

Finish Time: ....

Ascent Duration: ....

Descent Duration: ....

Total Time: ....

Total Distance Covered: ....

Weather Conditions: ☀ ⛅ ☁ 🌦 🌧 ❄

Temperature: .... ○ ○ ○ ○ ○ ○

Wind: ....

(poor) (great)
Difficulty: ○ ○ ○ ○ ○ ○ ○ ○ ○

Fufillment: ○ ○ ○ ○ ○ ○ ○ ○ ○

Scenery: ○ ○ ○ ○ ○ ○ ○ ○ ○

Companions: ....

....

....

....

Notes/Photos:

Beinn Liath Mhor Fannaich

Height: 954m
Grid Ref: NH 21962 72398

Date: ----------------------------------
Ascent Start Time: --------------------
Descent Start Time: ------------------
Peak Time: ----------------------------
Finish Time: --------------------------
Ascent Duration: ----------------------
Descent Duration: ---------------------
Total Time: ---------------------------
Total Distance Covered: ---------------
Weather Conditions:
Temperature: ------------
Wind: -----------

Difficulty: (poor) ○ ○ ○ ○ ○ ○ ○ ○ ○ (great)
Fufillment: ○ ○ ○ ○ ○ ○ ○ ○ ○
Scenery: ○ ○ ○ ○ ○ ○ ○ ○ ○
Companions: -------------------

Notes/Photos:

Am Faochagach

Height: 954m
Grid Ref: NH 30363 79360

Date: ------------------------------------
Ascent Start Time: ----------------------
Descent Start Time: ---------------------
Peak Time: ------------------------------
Finish Time: ----------------------------
Ascent Duration: ------------------------
Descent Duration: -----------------------
Total Time: -----------------------------
Total Distance Covered: -----------------
Weather Conditions: ☀ ⛅ ☁ 🌧 🌦 ❄
Temperature: --------- ○ ○ ○ ○ ○ ○
Wind: -----------

Difficulty: (poor) ○ ○ ○ ○ ○ ○ ○ ○ ○ ○ (great)
Fufillment: ○ ○ ○ ○ ○ ○ ○ ○ ○ ○
Scenery: ○ ○ ○ ○ ○ ○ ○ ○ ○ ○
Companions: -------------------

Notes/Photos:

Sgor Gaibhre

Height: 955m
Grid Ref: NN 44480 67439

Date: ....
Ascent Start Time: ....
Descent Start Time: ....
Peak Time: ....
Finish Time: ....
Ascent Duration: ....
Descent Duration: ....
Total Time: ....
Total Distance Covered: ....
Weather Conditions:
Temperature: ....
Wind: ....

(poor) (great)
Difficulty: ○ ○ ○ ○ ○ ○ ○ ○ ○
Fufillment: ○ ○ ○ ○ ○ ○ ○ ○ ○
Scenery: ○ ○ ○ ○ ○ ○ ○ ○ ○
Companions: ....
....
....
....

Notes/Photos:

Buachaille Etive Mor - Stob na Broige

Height: 956m
Grid Ref: NN 19076 52559

Date: ----

Ascent Start Time: ----

Descent Start Time: ----

Peak Time: ----

Finish Time: ----

Ascent Duration: ----

Descent Duration: ----

Total Time: ----

Total Distance Covered: ----

Weather Conditions:

Temperature: ----

Wind: ----

Difficulty: (poor) ○ ○ ○ ○ ○ ○ ○ ○ ○ (great)

Fufillment: ○ ○ ○ ○ ○ ○ ○ ○ ○

Scenery: ○ ○ ○ ○ ○ ○ ○ ○ ○

Companions: ----

Notes/Photos:

Saileag
Height: 956m
Grid Ref: NH 01777 14816

Date: ----------------------------------

Ascent Start Time: --------------------

Descent Start Time: -------------------

Peak Time: ----------------------------

Finish Time: --------------------------

Ascent Duration: ----------------------

Descent Duration: ---------------------

Total Time: ---------------------------

Total Distance Covered: ---------------

Weather Conditions:

Temperature: ---------

Wind: ----------

Difficulty: (poor) ○ ○ ○ ○ ○ ○ ○ ○ ○ (great)

Fufillment: ○ ○ ○ ○ ○ ○ ○ ○ ○

Scenery: ○ ○ ○ ○ ○ ○ ○ ○ ○

Companions: ---------------

Notes/Photos:

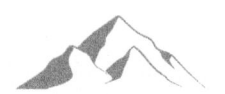

Sgurr nan Coireachan

Height: 956m
Grid Ref: NM 90294 88003

Date: ----------------------------------
Ascent Start Time: --------------------
Descent Start Time: ------------------
Peak Time: ----------------------------
Finish Time: --------------------------
Ascent Duration: ----------------------
Descent Duration: --------------------
Total Time: ---------------------------
Total Distance Covered: --------------
Weather Conditions: ☀ ⛅ ☁ 🌧 ⛈ ❄
Temperature: --------- ○ ○ ○ ○ ○ ○
Wind: -----------

(poor) (great)
Difficulty: ○ ○ ○ ○ ○ ○ ○ ○ ○
Fufillment: ○ ○ ○ ○ ○ ○ ○ ○ ○
Scenery: ○ ○ ○ ○ ○ ○ ○ ○ ○
Companions: ----------------

Notes/Photos:

Carn Ghluasaid

Height: 957m
Grid Ref: NH 14579 12513

Date: ----------------------------------

Ascent Start Time: --------------------

Descent Start Time: -------------------

Peak Time: ----------------------------

Finish Time: --------------------------

Ascent Duration: ----------------------

Descent Duration: ---------------------

Total Time: ---------------------------

Total Distance Covered: ---------------

Weather Conditions:

Temperature: ---------

Wind: ----------

(poor) (great)
Difficulty: ○ ○ ○ ○ ○ ○ ○ ○ ○ ○

Fufillment: ○ ○ ○ ○ ○ ○ ○ ○ ○ ○

Scenery: ○ ○ ○ ○ ○ ○ ○ ○ ○ ○

Companions: ----------------

Notes/Photos:

Tom Buidhe

Height: 957m
Grid Ref: NO 21368 78765

Date: ----------------------------------
Ascent Start Time: --------------------
Descent Start Time: -------------------
Peak Time: ----------------------------
Finish Time: --------------------------
Ascent Duration: ----------------------
Descent Duration: ---------------------
Total Time: ---------------------------
Total Distance Covered: ---------------
Weather Conditions: ☀️ ⛅ ☁️ 🌧️ 🌦️ ❄️
Temperature: ------- ○ ○ ○ ○ ○ ○
Wind: ----------

Difficulty: (poor) ○ ○ ○ ○ ○ ○ ○ ○ ○ ○ (great)
Fufillment: ○ ○ ○ ○ ○ ○ ○ ○ ○ ○
Scenery: ○ ○ ○ ○ ○ ○ ○ ○ ○ ○
Companions: -----------------

Notes/Photos:

Bruach na Frithe

Height: 958m
Grid Ref: NG 46090 25186

Date: ----------------------------------
Ascent Start Time: --------------------
Descent Start Time: -------------------
Peak Time: -----------------------------
Finish Time: ---------------------------
Ascent Duration: -----------------------
Descent Duration: ----------------------
Total Time: ----------------------------
Total Distance Covered: ---------------
Weather Conditions: ☀ ⛅ ☁ 🌧 ⛈ ❄
Temperature: --------- ○ ○ ○ ○ ○ ○
Wind: -----------

(poor) (great)
Difficulty: ○ ○ ○ ○ ○ ○ ○ ○ ○
Fufillment: ○ ○ ○ ○ ○ ○ ○ ○ ○
Scenery: ○ ○ ○ ○ ○ ○ ○ ○ ○
Companions: -----------------

Notes/Photos:

Buachaille Etive Beag - Stob Dubh

Height: 958m
Grid Ref: NN 17914 53532

Date: ----------------------------------

Ascent Start Time: ---------------------

Descent Start Time: --------------------

Peak Time: -----------------------------

Finish Time: ---------------------------

Ascent Duration: -----------------------

Descent Duration: ----------------------

Total Time: ----------------------------

Total Distance Covered: ----------------

Weather Conditions:

Temperature: ○ ○ ○ ○ ○ ○

Wind: ----------

(poor) (great)
Difficulty: ○ ○ ○ ○ ○ ○ ○ ○ ○

Fufillment: ○ ○ ○ ○ ○ ○ ○ ○ ○

Scenery: ○ ○ ○ ○ ○ ○ ○ ○ ○

Companions: ----------------

Notes/Photos:

Tolmount

Height: 958m
Grid Ref: NO 21052 80009

Date: ....

Ascent Start Time: ....

Descent Start Time: ....

Peak Time: ....

Finish Time: ....

Ascent Duration: ....

Descent Duration: ....

Total Time: ....

Total Distance Covered: ....

Weather Conditions: ☀ ⛅ ☁ 🌧 🌦 ❄

Temperature: .... ○ ○ ○ ○ ○ ○

Wind: ....

(poor) (great)
Difficulty: ○ ○ ○ ○ ○ ○ ○ ○ ○ ○

Fufillment: ○ ○ ○ ○ ○ ○ ○ ○ ○ ○

Scenery: ○ ○ ○ ○ ○ ○ ○ ○ ○ ○

Companions: ....

....

....

....

Notes/Photos:

Beinn Fhionnlaidh

Height: 959m
Grid Ref: NN 09512 49760

Date: ----------------------------------

Ascent Start Time: ---------------------

Descent Start Time: --------------------

Peak Time: -----------------------------

Finish Time: ---------------------------

Ascent Duration: -----------------------

Descent Duration: ----------------------

Total Time: ----------------------------

Total Distance Covered: ---------------

Weather Conditions: ☀ ⛅ ☁ 🌧 ☔ ❄

Temperature: --------- ○ ○ ○ ○ ○ ○

Wind: -----------

(poor) (great)
Difficulty: ○ ○ ○ ○ ○ ○ ○ ○ ○

Fufillment: ○ ○ ○ ○ ○ ○ ○ ○ ○

Scenery: ○ ○ ○ ○ ○ ○ ○ ○ ○

Companions: -----------------

Notes/Photos:

Meall Glas

Height: 959m
Grid Ref: NN 43151 32186

Date: ----------------------------------

Ascent Start Time: --------------------

Descent Start Time: -------------------

Peak Time: ------------------------------

Finish Time: ----------------------------

Ascent Duration: -----------------------

Descent Duration: ----------------------

Total Time: -----------------------------

Total Distance Covered: ---------------

Weather Conditions: ☀ ⛅ ☁ 🌧 🌦 ❄

Temperature: --------- ○ ○ ○ ○ ○ ○

Wind: ----------

	(poor)	(great)
Difficulty:	○ ○ ○ ○ ○ ○ ○ ○ ○ ○

Fufillment: ○ ○ ○ ○ ○ ○ ○ ○ ○ ○

Scenery: ○ ○ ○ ○ ○ ○ ○ ○ ○ ○

Companions: ------------------

Notes/Photos:

Beinn nan Aighenan

Height: 960m
Grid Ref: NN 14855 40520

Date: ----------------------------------

Ascent Start Time: ---------------------

Descent Start Time: --------------------

Peak Time: -----------------------------

Finish Time: ---------------------------

Ascent Duration: -----------------------

Descent Duration: ----------------------

Total Time: ----------------------------

Total Distance Covered: ----------------

Weather Conditions:

Temperature: ---------

Wind: -----------

(poor) (great)
Difficulty: ○ ○ ○ ○ ○ ○ ○ ○ ○ ○

Fufillment: ○ ○ ○ ○ ○ ○ ○ ○ ○ ○

Scenery: ○ ○ ○ ○ ○ ○ ○ ○ ○ ○

Companions: ----------------

Notes/Photos:

Stuchd an Lochain

Height: 960m
Grid Ref: NN 48308 44832

Date: ----
Ascent Start Time: ----
Descent Start Time: ----
Peak Time: ----
Finish Time: ----
Ascent Duration: ----
Descent Duration: ----
Total Time: ----
Total Distance Covered: ----
Weather Conditions:
Temperature: ----
Wind: ----

(poor) (great)
Difficulty: ○ ○ ○ ○ ○ ○ ○ ○ ○
Fufillment: ○ ○ ○ ○ ○ ○ ○ ○ ○
Scenery: ○ ○ ○ ○ ○ ○ ○ ○ ○
Companions: ----

Notes/Photos:

Sgorr Ruadh

Height: 961m
Grid Ref: NG 95910 50494

Date: ------------------------------

Ascent Start Time: --------------------

Descent Start Time: ------------------

Peak Time: ---------------------------

Finish Time: -------------------------

Ascent Duration: ---------------------

Descent Duration: --------------------

Total Time: --------------------------

Total Distance Covered: --------------

Weather Conditions: ☀ ⛅ ☁ 🌧 🌦 ❄

Temperature: --------- ○ ○ ○ ○ ○ ○

Wind: -----------

(poor)　　　　　　　(great)
Difficulty: ○ ○ ○ ○ ○ ○ ○ ○ ○

Fufillment: ○ ○ ○ ○ ○ ○ ○ ○ ○

Scenery: ○ ○ ○ ○ ○ ○ ○ ○ ○

Companions: ----------------

Notes/Photos:

Ben Klibreck - Meall nan Con

Height: 962m
Grid Ref: NC 58531 29908

Date: ----------
Ascent Start Time: ----------
Descent Start Time: ----------
Peak Time: ----------
Finish Time: ----------
Ascent Duration: ----------
Descent Duration: ----------
Total Time: ----------
Total Distance Covered: ----------
Weather Conditions:
Temperature: ----------
Wind: ----------

(poor) (great)
Difficulty: ○ ○ ○ ○ ○ ○ ○ ○ ○
Fufillment: ○ ○ ○ ○ ○ ○ ○ ○ ○
Scenery: ○ ○ ○ ○ ○ ○ ○ ○ ○
Companions: ----------

Notes/Photos:

Carn a'Chlamain

Height: 963m
Grid Ref: NN 91592 75798

Date: ----------------------------------

Ascent Start Time: --------------------

Descent Start Time: -------------------

Peak Time: ----------------------------

Finish Time: --------------------------

Ascent Duration: ----------------------

Descent Duration: ---------------------

Total Time: ---------------------------

Total Distance Covered: --------------

Weather Conditions:

Temperature: ---------

Wind: -----------

(poor) (great)
Difficulty: ○ ○ ○ ○ ○ ○ ○ ○ ○ ○

Fufillment: ○ ○ ○ ○ ○ ○ ○ ○ ○ ○

Scenery: ○ ○ ○ ○ ○ ○ ○ ○ ○ ○

Companions: ----------------

Notes/Photos:

Sgurr Thuilm

Height: 963m
Grid Ref: NM 93910 87970

Date: ----------------------------------
Ascent Start Time: --------------------
Descent Start Time: -------------------
Peak Time: ----------------------------
Finish Time: --------------------------
Ascent Duration: ----------------------
Descent Duration: ---------------------
Total Time: ---------------------------
Total Distance Covered: ---------------
Weather Conditions:
Temperature: ---------
Wind: -----------

(poor) (great)
Difficulty: ○ ○ ○ ○ ○ ○ ○ ○ ○
Fufillment: ○ ○ ○ ○ ○ ○ ○ ○ ○
Scenery: ○ ○ ○ ○ ○ ○ ○ ○ ○
Companions: ---------------

Notes/Photos:

Sgurr nan Gillean

Height: 964m
Grid Ref: NG 47162 25284

Date: ---------------------------------
Ascent Start Time: --------------------
Descent Start Time: -------------------
Peak Time: ----------------------------
Finish Time: --------------------------
Ascent Duration: ----------------------
Descent Duration: ---------------------
Total Time: ---------------------------
Total Distance Covered: ---------------
Weather Conditions:
Temperature: --------- ○ ○ ○ ○ ○ ○
Wind: ----------

(poor) (great)
Difficulty: ○ ○ ○ ○ ○ ○ ○ ○ ○ ○
Fufillment: ○ ○ ○ ○ ○ ○ ○ ○ ○ ○
Scenery: ○ ○ ○ ○ ○ ○ ○ ○ ○ ○
Companions: ----------------

Notes/Photos:

Sgurr na Banachdich

Height: 965m
Grid Ref: NG 44112 22280

Date: ----------------------------------
Ascent Start Time: --------------------
Descent Start Time: -------------------
Peak Time: ----------------------------
Finish Time: --------------------------
Ascent Duration: ----------------------
Descent Duration: ---------------------
Total Time: ---------------------------
Total Distance Covered: ---------------
Weather Conditions: ☀ ⛅ ☁ 🌦 🌧 ❄
Temperature: --------- ○ ○ ○ ○ ○ ○
Wind: ----------

Difficulty: (poor) ○ ○ ○ ○ ○ ○ ○ ○ ○ (great)
Fufillment: ○ ○ ○ ○ ○ ○ ○ ○ ○
Scenery: ○ ○ ○ ○ ○ ○ ○ ○ ○
Companions: -----------------

Notes/Photos:

Ben More
Height: 966m
Grid Ref: NM 52582 33069

Date: -------------------------------

Ascent Start Time: -------------------

Descent Start Time: ------------------

Peak Time: ---------------------------

Finish Time: -------------------------

Ascent Duration: ---------------------

Descent Duration: --------------------

Total Time: --------------------------

Total Distance Covered: --------------

Weather Conditions: ☀ ⛅ ☁ 🌧 ⛆ ❄

Temperature: --------- ○ ○ ○ ○ ○ ○

Wind: ----------

(poor) (great)
Difficulty: ○ ○ ○ ○ ○ ○ ○ ○ ○ ○

Fufillment: ○ ○ ○ ○ ○ ○ ○ ○ ○ ○

Scenery: ○ ○ ○ ○ ○ ○ ○ ○ ○ ○

Companions: ----------------

Notes/Photos:

A'Mhaighdean

Height: 967m
Grid Ref: NH 00779 74901

Date: ----------------------------
Ascent Start Time: -------------------
Descent Start Time: ------------------
Peak Time: ------------------------
Finish Time: -----------------------
Ascent Duration: --------------------
Descent Duration: -------------------
Total Time: ------------------------
Total Distance Covered: --------------
Weather Conditions:
Temperature: ----------
Wind: ----------

Difficulty: (poor) ○ ○ ○ ○ ○ ○ ○ ○ ○ (great)
Fufillment: ○ ○ ○ ○ ○ ○ ○ ○ ○
Scenery: ○ ○ ○ ○ ○ ○ ○ ○ ○
Companions: -----------------

Notes/Photos:

Aonach Eagach - Sgorr nam Fiannaidh

Height: 967m
Grid Ref: NN 14048 58295

Date: ....
Ascent Start Time: ....
Descent Start Time: ....
Peak Time: ....
Finish Time: ....
Ascent Duration: ....
Descent Duration: ....
Total Time: ....
Total Distance Covered: ....
Weather Conditions: ☀ ⛅ ☁ 🌧 💧 ❄
Temperature: .... ○ ○ ○ ○ ○ ○
Wind: ....

(poor) (great)
Difficulty: ○ ○ ○ ○ ○ ○ ○ ○ ○
Fufillment: ○ ○ ○ ○ ○ ○ ○ ○ ○
Scenery: ○ ○ ○ ○ ○ ○ ○ ○ ○
Companions: ....

....
....
....

Notes/Photos:

Meall Garbh

Height: 968m
Grid Ref: NN 64709 51678

Date: ---
Ascent Start Time: ---
Descent Start Time: ---
Peak Time: ---
Finish Time: ---
Ascent Duration: ---
Descent Duration: ---
Total Time: ---
Total Distance Covered: ---
Weather Conditions:
Temperature: ---
Wind: ---

(poor) (great)
Difficulty: ○ ○ ○ ○ ○ ○ ○ ○ ○
Fufillment: ○ ○ ○ ○ ○ ○ ○ ○ ○
Scenery: ○ ○ ○ ○ ○ ○ ○ ○ ○
Companions: ---

Notes/Photos:

Sgurr a'Ghreadaidh

Height: 972m
Grid Ref: NG 44530 23114

Date: ----------------------------------
Ascent Start Time: --------------------
Descent Start Time: -------------------
Peak Time: ----------------------------
Finish Time: --------------------------
Ascent Duration: ----------------------
Descent Duration: ---------------------
Total Time: ---------------------------
Total Distance Covered: ---------------
Weather Conditions: ☀ ⛅ ☁ 🌧 🌦 ❄
Temperature: --------- ○ ○ ○ ○ ○ ○
Wind: -----------

(poor) (great)
Difficulty: ○ ○ ○ ○ ○ ○ ○ ○ ○
Fufillment: ○ ○ ○ ○ ○ ○ ○ ○ ○
Scenery: ○ ○ ○ ○ ○ ○ ○ ○ ○
Companions: ------------------

Notes/Photos:

1hr 1G Stirling

Ben Lomond FK8 3TR
Height: 973m
Grid Ref: NN 36711 02856

Ascent Start Time: _____
Descent Start Time: _____
Peak Time: _____
Finish Time: _____
Ascent Duration: _____
Descent Duration: _____
Total Time: _____
Total Distance Covered: _____
Weather Conditions: ☀ ⛅ ☁ 🌧 ⛈ ❄
Temperature: _____ ○ ○ ○ ○ ○ ○
Wind: _____

Difficulty: (poor) ○ ○ ○ ○ ○ ○ ○ ○ ○ (great)
Fufillment: ○ ○ ○ ○ ○ ○ ○ ○ ○
Scenery: ○ ○ ○ ○ ○ ○ ○ ○ ○
Companions: _____
_____
_____
_____

Notes/Photos:

Stuc a'Chroin

Height: 974m
Grid Ref: NN 61749 17458

Date: ------------------------------------

Ascent Start Time: ---------------------

Descent Start Time: --------------------

Peak Time: ---------------------------

Finish Time: --------------------------

Ascent Duration: ----------------------

Descent Duration: ---------------------

Total Time: ---------------------------

Total Distance Covered: --------------

Weather Conditions: ☀ ⛅ ☁ 🌧 ⛈ ❄

Temperature: -------- ○ ○ ○ ○ ○ ○

Wind: ----------

(poor) (great)
Difficulty: ○ ○ ○ ○ ○ ○ ○ ○ ○ ○

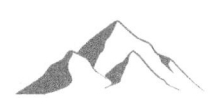

Fufillment: ○ ○ ○ ○ ○ ○ ○ ○ ○ ○

Scenery: ○ ○ ○ ○ ○ ○ ○ ○ ○ ○

Companions: ------------------

Notes/Photos:

Beinn Sgritheall

Height: 974m
Grid Ref: NG 83592 12671

Date: ----------------------------
Ascent Start Time: -------------------
Descent Start Time: ------------------
Peak Time: ---------------------------
Finish Time: -------------------------
Ascent Duration: ---------------------
Descent Duration: --------------------
Total Time: --------------------------
Total Distance Covered: --------------
Weather Conditions:
Temperature: ---------
Wind: -----------

(poor) (great)
Difficulty: ○ ○ ○ ○ ○ ○ ○ ○ ○
Fufillment: ○ ○ ○ ○ ○ ○ ○ ○ ○
Scenery: ○ ○ ○ ○ ○ ○ ○ ○ ○
Companions: ---------------

Notes/Photos:

Stob Ban

Height: 975m
Grid Ref: NN 26672 72386

Date: ....
Ascent Start Time: ....
Descent Start Time: ....
Peak Time: ....
Finish Time: ....
Ascent Duration: ....
Descent Duration: ....
Total Time: ....
Total Distance Covered: ....
Weather Conditions: ☀️ ⛅ ☁️ 🌧️ 🌦️ ❄️
Temperature: .... ○ ○ ○ ○ ○ ○
Wind: ....

(poor) (great)
Difficulty: ○ ○ ○ ○ ○ ○ ○ ○ ○
Fufillment: ○ ○ ○ ○ ○ ○ ○ ○ ○
Scenery: ○ ○ ○ ○ ○ ○ ○ ○ ○
Companions: ....
....
....
....

Notes/Photos:

A'Mharconaich

Height: 975m
Grid Ref: NN 60425 76284

Date: ----------------------------------

Ascent Start Time: --------------------

Descent Start Time: -------------------

Peak Time: -----------------------------

Finish Time: ---------------------------

Ascent Duration: -----------------------

Descent Duration: ----------------------

Total Time: ----------------------------

Total Distance Covered: ---------------

Weather Conditions:

Temperature: --------- ○ ○ ○ ○ ○ ○

Wind: -----------

(poor) (great)
Difficulty: ○ ○ ○ ○ ○ ○ ○ ○ ○

Fufillment: ○ ○ ○ ○ ○ ○ ○ ○ ○

Scenery: ○ ○ ○ ○ ○ ○ ○ ○ ○

Companions: --------------------

Notes/Photos:

Carn a'Gheoidh

Height: 975m
Grid Ref: NO 10704 76692

Date: ---------------------------------
Ascent Start Time: --------------------
Descent Start Time: -------------------
Peak Time: ----------------------------
Finish Time: --------------------------
Ascent Duration: ----------------------
Descent Duration: ---------------------
Total Time: ---------------------------
Total Distance Covered: ---------------
Weather Conditions: ☼ ⛅ ☁ 🌧 ❄
Temperature: --------- ○ ○ ○ ○ ○ ○
Wind: -----------

(poor) (great)
Difficulty: ○ ○ ○ ○ ○ ○ ○ ○ ○ ○
Fufillment: ○ ○ ○ ○ ○ ○ ○ ○ ○ ○
Scenery: ○ ○ ○ ○ ○ ○ ○ ○ ○ ○
Companions: ---------------

Notes/Photos:

Beinn a'Ghlo - Carn Liath

Height: 975m
Grid Ref: NN 93608 69822

Date: _____

Ascent Start Time: _____

Descent Start Time: _____

Peak Time: _____

Finish Time: _____

Ascent Duration: _____

Descent Duration: _____

Total Time: _____

Total Distance Covered: _____

Weather Conditions:

Temperature: _____ ○ ○ ○ ○ ○ ○

Wind: _____

(poor) (great)
Difficulty: ○ ○ ○ ○ ○ ○ ○ ○ ○

Fufillment: ○ ○ ○ ○ ○ ○ ○ ○ ○

Scenery: ○ ○ ○ ○ ○ ○ ○ ○ ○

Companions: _____
_____
_____
_____

Notes/Photos:

Cona' Mheall

Height: 977m
Grid Ref: NH 27511 81630

Date: ----------------------------------
Ascent Start Time: --------------------
Descent Start Time: -------------------
Peak Time: ----------------------------
Finish Time: ---------------------------
Ascent Duration: -----------------------
Descent Duration: ----------------------
Total Time: ----------------------------
Total Distance Covered: ---------------
Weather Conditions:
Temperature: ---------
Wind: ----------

(poor) (great)
Difficulty: ○ ○ ○ ○ ○ ○ ○ ○ ○
Fufillment: ○ ○ ○ ○ ○ ○ ○ ○ ○
Scenery: ○ ○ ○ ○ ○ ○ ○ ○ ○
Companions: ------------------

Notes/Photos:

Meall nan Ceapraichean

Height: 977m
Grid Ref: NH 25729 82536

Date: ------------------------------

Ascent Start Time: --------------------

Descent Start Time: ------------------

Peak Time: ---------------------------

Finish Time: -------------------------

Ascent Duration: ---------------------

Descent Duration: --------------------

Total Time: --------------------------

Total Distance Covered: --------------

Weather Conditions:

Temperature: ---------

Wind: ----------

(poor) (great)
Difficulty: ○ ○ ○ ○ ○ ○ ○ ○ ○

Fufillment: ○ ○ ○ ○ ○ ○ ○ ○ ○

Scenery: ○ ○ ○ ○ ○ ○ ○ ○ ○

Companions: ------------------

Notes/Photos:

Stob Coire Sgriodain

Height: 978m
Grid Ref: NN 35672 74372

Date: ----------------------------------
Ascent Start Time: --------------------
Descent Start Time: -------------------
Peak Time: ----------------------------
Finish Time: --------------------------
Ascent Duration: ----------------------
Descent Duration: ---------------------
Total Time: ---------------------------
Total Distance Covered: ---------------
Weather Conditions: ☀ ⛅ ☁ 🌧 ☔ ❄
Temperature: ---------- ○ ○ ○ ○ ○ ○
Wind: ----------

Difficulty: (poor) ○ ○ ○ ○ ○ ○ ○ ○ ○ ○ (great)
Fufillment: ○ ○ ○ ○ ○ ○ ○ ○ ○ ○
Scenery: ○ ○ ○ ○ ○ ○ ○ ○ ○ ○
Companions: ---------------

Notes/Photos:

Beinn Dubhchraig

Height: 978m
Grid Ref: NN 30767 25485

Date: ----------------------------------
Ascent Start Time: --------------------
Descent Start Time: -------------------
Peak Time: -----------------------------
Finish Time: ---------------------------
Ascent Duration: -----------------------
Descent Duration: ----------------------
Total Time: ----------------------------
Total Distance Covered: ----------------
Weather Conditions:
Temperature: ----------
Wind: ----------

(poor) (great)
Difficulty: ○ ○ ○ ○ ○ ○ ○ ○ ○ ○
Fufillment: ○ ○ ○ ○ ○ ○ ○ ○ ○ ○
Scenery: ○ ○ ○ ○ ○ ○ ○ ○ ○ ○
Companions: ----------------

Notes/Photos:

Beinn a'Chochuill

Height: 979m
Grid Ref: NN 10982 32840

Date: ----------------------------------
Ascent Start Time: --------------------
Descent Start Time: ------------------
Peak Time: ---------------------------
Finish Time: --------------------------
Ascent Duration: ---------------------
Descent Duration: --------------------
Total Time: ---------------------------
Total Distance Covered: -------------
Weather Conditions: ☀ ⛅ ☁ 🌧 🌬 ❄
Temperature: -------- ○ ○ ○ ○ ○ ○
Wind: -----------

(poor) (great)
Difficulty: ○ ○ ○ ○ ○ ○ ○ ○ ○ ○
Fufillment: ○ ○ ○ ○ ○ ○ ○ ○ ○ ○
Scenery: ○ ○ ○ ○ ○ ○ ○ ○ ○ ○
Companions: ----------------

Notes/Photos:

Ciste Dhubh

Height: 979m
Grid Ref: NH 06239 16607

Date: ----------------------------------
Ascent Start Time: --------------------
Descent Start Time: -------------------
Peak Time: ----------------------------
Finish Time: --------------------------
Ascent Duration: ----------------------
Descent Duration: ---------------------
Total Time: ---------------------------
Total Distance Covered: ---------------
Weather Conditions:
Temperature: --------
Wind: ----------

(poor) (great)
Difficulty: ○ ○ ○ ○ ○ ○ ○ ○ ○
Fufillment: ○ ○ ○ ○ ○ ○ ○ ○ ○
Scenery: ○ ○ ○ ○ ○ ○ ○ ○ ○
Companions: -----------------

Notes/Photos:

Stob Coire a'Chairn

Height: 980m
Grid Ref: NN 18565 66054

Date: ---------------------------------
Ascent Start Time: --------------------
Descent Start Time: -------------------
Peak Time: ----------------------------
Finish Time: --------------------------
Ascent Duration: ----------------------
Descent Duration: ---------------------
Total Time: ---------------------------
Total Distance Covered: ---------------
Weather Conditions: ☀ ⛅ ☁ 🌧 ❄ ❆
Temperature: -------- ○ ○ ○ ○ ○ ○
Wind: -----------

                (poor)   (great)
Difficulty: ○ ○ ○ ○ ○ ○ ○ ○ ○ ○
Fufillment: ○ ○ ○ ○ ○ ○ ○ ○ ○ ○
Scenery: ○ ○ ○ ○ ○ ○ ○ ○ ○ ○
Companions: ----------------

Notes/Photos:

Mullach na Dheiragain

Height: 981m
Grid Ref: NH 08047 25906

Date: ----------------------------------

Ascent Start Time: --------------------

Descent Start Time: -------------------

Peak Time: ------------------------------

Finish Time: ----------------------------

Ascent Duration: -----------------------

Descent Duration: ----------------------

Total Time: ------------------------------

Total Distance Covered: --------------

Weather Conditions:

Temperature: ---------- ○ ○ ○ ○ ○ ○

Wind: -----------

(poor) (great)
Difficulty: ○ ○ ○ ○ ○ ○ ○ ○ ○ ○

Fufillment: ○ ○ ○ ○ ○ ○ ○ ○ ○ ○

Scenery: ○ ○ ○ ○ ○ ○ ○ ○ ○ ○

Companions: ---------------------

Notes/Photos:

Maol Chinn-dearg

Height: 981m
Grid Ref: NN 69479 49661

Date: ----------------------------------
Ascent Start Time: --------------------
Descent Start Time: -------------------
Peak Time: ----------------------------
Finish Time: --------------------------
Ascent Duration: ----------------------
Descent Duration: ---------------------
Total Time: ---------------------------
Total Distance Covered: ---------------
Weather Conditions: ☀ ⛅ ☁ 🌧 ⛈ ❄
Temperature: -------- ○ ○ ○ ○ ○ ○
Wind: ----------

(poor) (great)
Difficulty: ○ ○ ○ ○ ○ ○ ○ ○ ○
Fufillment: ○ ○ ○ ○ ○ ○ ○ ○ ○
Scenery: ○ ○ ○ ○ ○ ○ ○ ○ ○
Companions: ------------------

Notes/Photos:

Meall na Aighean
Height: 981m
Grid Ref: NN 69479 49661

Date: ....

Ascent Start Time: ....

Descent Start Time: ....

Peak Time: ....

Finish Time: ....

Ascent Duration: ....

Descent Duration: ....

Total Time: ....

Total Distance Covered: ....

Weather Conditions: ☀ ⛅ ☁ 🌧 ⛈ ❄

Temperature: .... ○ ○ ○ ○ ○ ○

Wind: ....

(poor) (great)
Difficulty: ○ ○ ○ ○ ○ ○ ○ ○ ○

Fufillment: ○ ○ ○ ○ ○ ○ ○ ○ ○

Scenery: ○ ○ ○ ○ ○ ○ ○ ○ ○

Companions: ....

....

....

....

Notes/Photos:

Slioch
Height: 981m
Grid Ref:NH 00471 69064

Date: ------------------------------
Ascent Start Time: --------------------
Descent Start Time: ------------------
Peak Time: ---------------------------
Finish Time: -------------------------
Ascent Duration: ----------------------
Descent Duration: ---------------------
Total Time: --------------------------
Total Distance Covered: --------------
Weather Conditions: ☀ ⛅ ☁ 🌧 ⛈ ❄
Temperature: --------- ○ ○ ○ ○ ○ ○
Wind: -----------

(poor)   (great)
Difficulty: ○ ○ ○ ○ ○ ○ ○ ○ ○
Fufillment: ○ ○ ○ ○ ○ ○ ○ ○ ○
Scenery: ○ ○ ○ ○ ○ ○ ○ ○ ○
Companions: -----------------

Notes/Photos:

Ben Vorlich

Height: 982m
Grid Ref: NN 62915 18909

Date: _____

Ascent Start Time: _____

Descent Start Time: _____

Peak Time: _____

Finish Time: _____

Ascent Duration: _____

Descent Duration: _____

Total Time: _____

Total Distance Covered: _____

Weather Conditions:

Temperature: _____ ○ ○ ○ ○ ○ ○

Wind: _____

(poor) (great)
Difficulty: ○ ○ ○ ○ ○ ○ ○ ○ ○

Fufillment: ○ ○ ○ ○ ○ ○ ○ ○ ○

Scenery: ○ ○ ○ ○ ○ ○ ○ ○ ○

Companions: _____

_____

_____

_____

Notes/Photos:

An Gearanach

Height: 982m
Grid Ref: NN 18774 66983

Date: ----------------------------------

Ascent Start Time: --------------------

Descent Start Time: -------------------

Peak Time: ----------------------------

Finish Time: --------------------------

Ascent Duration: ----------------------

Descent Duration: ---------------------

Total Time: ---------------------------

Total Distance Covered: ---------------

Weather Conditions: ☀ ⛅ ☁ 🌧 🌫 ❄

Temperature: --------- ○ ○ ○ ○ ○ ○

Wind: ----------

(poor) (great)
Difficulty: ○ ○ ○ ○ ○ ○ ○ ○ ○ ○

Fufillment: ○ ○ ○ ○ ○ ○ ○ ○ ○ ○

Scenery: ○ ○ ○ ○ ○ ○ ○ ○ ○ ○

Companions: ---------------

Notes/Photos:

Sgurr Dearg - Inaccessible Pinnacle

Height: 985m
Grid Ref: NG 44409 21552

Date: ....

Ascent Start Time: ....

Descent Start Time: ....

Peak Time: ....

Finish Time: ....

Ascent Duration: ....

Descent Duration: ....

Total Time: ....

Total Distance Covered: ....

Weather Conditions:

Temperature: .... ○ ○ ○ ○ ○ ○

Wind: ....

(poor)　　　　　(great)
Difficulty: ○ ○ ○ ○ ○ ○ ○ ○ ○

Fufillment: ○ ○ ○ ○ ○ ○ ○ ○ ○

Scenery: ○ ○ ○ ○ ○ ○ ○ ○ ○

Companions: ....

Notes/Photos:

Gulvain [Gaor Bheinn]
Height: 986m
Grid Ref: NN 00272 87565

Date: ----------------------------------

Ascent Start Time: --------------------

Descent Start Time: -------------------

Peak Time: ----------------------------

Finish Time: --------------------------

Ascent Duration: ----------------------

Descent Duration: ---------------------

Total Time: ---------------------------

Total Distance Covered: ---------------

Weather Conditions:

Temperature: ---------

Wind: ----------

(poor) (great)
Difficulty: ○ ○ ○ ○ ○ ○ ○ ○ ○

Fufillment: ○ ○ ○ ○ ○ ○ ○ ○ ○

Scenery: ○ ○ ○ ○ ○ ○ ○ ○ ○

Companions: ----------------

Notes/Photos:

Beinn Alligin - Sgurr Mhor

Height: 986m
Grid Ref: NG 86568 61258

Date: ----------------------------------
Ascent Start Time: --------------------
Descent Start Time: -------------------
Peak Time: ----------------------------
Finish Time: --------------------------
Ascent Duration: ----------------------
Descent Duration: ---------------------
Total Time: ---------------------------
Total Distance Covered: ---------------
Weather Conditions:
Temperature: ---------
Wind: ----------

(poor) (great)
Difficulty: ○ ○ ○ ○ ○ ○ ○ ○ ○ ○
Fufillment: ○ ○ ○ ○ ○ ○ ○ ○ ○ ○
Scenery: ○ ○ ○ ○ ○ ○ ○ ○ ○ ○
Companions: ---------------

Notes/Photos:

Lurg Mhor
Height: 986m
Grid Ref: NH 06483 40440

Date: ---------------------------------

Ascent Start Time: --------------------

Descent Start Time: -------------------

Peak Time: ----------------------------

Finish Time: --------------------------

Ascent Duration: ----------------------

Descent Duration: ---------------------

Total Time: ---------------------------

Total Distance Covered: ---------------

Weather Conditions:

Temperature: ⚬ ⚬ ⚬ ⚬ ⚬ ⚬

Wind: ----------

(poor) (great)
Difficulty: ⚬ ⚬ ⚬ ⚬ ⚬ ⚬ ⚬ ⚬ ⚬ ⚬

Fufillment: ⚬ ⚬ ⚬ ⚬ ⚬ ⚬ ⚬ ⚬ ⚬ ⚬

Scenery: ⚬ ⚬ ⚬ ⚬ ⚬ ⚬ ⚬ ⚬ ⚬ ⚬

Companions: -----------------

Notes/Photos:

Sgurr Ban

Height: 987m
Grid Ref: NH 05584 74542

Date: ---------------------------------
Ascent Start Time: --------------------
Descent Start Time: -------------------
Peak Time: ---------------------------
Finish Time: --------------------------
Ascent Duration: ----------------------
Descent Duration: ---------------------
Total Time: ---------------------------
Total Distance Covered: ---------------
Weather Conditions:
Temperature: --------- ○ ○ ○ ○ ○ ○
Wind: ---------

(poor) (great)
Difficulty: ○ ○ ○ ○ ○ ○ ○ ○ ○
Fufillment: ○ ○ ○ ○ ○ ○ ○ ○ ○
Scenery: ○ ○ ○ ○ ○ ○ ○ ○ ○
Companions: -------------------

Notes/Photos:

Conival
Height: 987m
Grid Ref: NC 30332 19925

Date: ------------------------------

Ascent Start Time: -------------------

Descent Start Time: ------------------

Peak Time: ---------------------------

Finish Time: -------------------------

Ascent Duration: ---------------------

Descent Duration: --------------------

Total Time: --------------------------

Total Distance Covered: --------------

Weather Conditions: ☀ ⛅ ☁ 🌧 ☔ ❄

Temperature: --------- ○ ○ ○ ○ ○ ○

Wind: ----------

(poor) (great)
Difficulty: ○ ○ ○ ○ ○ ○ ○ ○ ○

Fufillment: ○ ○ ○ ○ ○ ○ ○ ○ ○

Scenery: ○ ○ ○ ○ ○ ○ ○ ○ ○

Companions: ----------------

Notes/Photos:

Creag Leacach
Height: 987m
Grid Ref: NO 15469 74540

Date: ----------------------------------

Ascent Start Time: --------------------

Descent Start Time: -------------------

Peak Time: ----------------------------

Finish Time: --------------------------

Ascent Duration: ----------------------

Descent Duration: ---------------------

Total Time: ---------------------------

Total Distance Covered: ---------------

Weather Conditions: ☀ ⛅ ☁ 🌧 🌦 ❄

Temperature: --------- ○ ○ ○ ○ ○ ○

Wind: ----------

(poor) (great)
Difficulty: ○ ○ ○ ○ ○ ○ ○ ○ ○ ○

Fufillment: ○ ○ ○ ○ ○ ○ ○ ○ ○ ○

Scenery: ○ ○ ○ ○ ○ ○ ○ ○ ○ ○

Companions: ---------------

Notes/Photos:

Druim Shionnach

Height: 987m
Grid Ref: NH 07444 08474

Date: ----------------------------------

Ascent Start Time: --------------------

Descent Start Time: -------------------

Peak Time: ----------------------------

Finish Time: --------------------------

Ascent Duration: ----------------------

Descent Duration: ---------------------

Total Time: ---------------------------

Total Distance Covered: ---------------

Weather Conditions:

Temperature: ---------

Wind: ----------

(poor) (great)
Difficulty: ○ ○ ○ ○ ○ ○ ○ ○ ○

Fufillment: ○ ○ ○ ○ ○ ○ ○ ○ ○

Scenery: ○ ○ ○ ○ ○ ○ ○ ○ ○

Companions: -------------------

Notes/Photos:

Sgairneach Mhor
Height: 989m
Grid Ref: NN 59884 73121

Date: ----------------------------------
Ascent Start Time: --------------------
Descent Start Time: -------------------
Peak Time: ----------------------------
Finish Time: --------------------------
Ascent Duration: ----------------------
Descent Duration: ---------------------
Total Time: ---------------------------
Total Distance Covered: ---------------
Weather Conditions: ☀ ⛅ ☁ 🌧 ⛈ ❄
Temperature: --------- ○ ○ ○ ○ ○ ○
Wind: -----------

(poor) (great)
Difficulty: ○ ○ ○ ○ ○ ○ ○ ○ ○
Fufillment: ○ ○ ○ ○ ○ ○ ○ ○ ○
Scenery: ○ ○ ○ ○ ○ ○ ○ ○ ○
Companions: -------------------

Notes/Photos:

Beinn Eunaich

Height: 989m
Grid Ref: NN 13566 32789

Date: _____

Ascent Start Time: _____

Descent Start Time: _____

Peak Time: _____

Finish Time: _____

Ascent Duration: _____

Descent Duration: _____

Total Time: _____

Total Distance Covered: _____

Weather Conditions: ☀️ ⛅ ☁️ 🌧️ ⛈️ ❄️

Temperature: _____ ○ ○ ○ ○ ○ ○

Wind: _____

(poor) (great)
Difficulty: ○ ○ ○ ○ ○ ○ ○ ○ ○

Fufillment: ○ ○ ○ ○ ○ ○ ○ ○ ○

Scenery: ○ ○ ○ ○ ○ ○ ○ ○ ○

Companions: _____

_____
_____
_____

Notes/Photos:

Sgurr Alasdair

Height: 991m
Grid Ref: NG 45005 20771

Date: ----------------------------------
Ascent Start Time: --------------------
Descent Start Time: -------------------
Peak Time: ----------------------------
Finish Time: --------------------------
Ascent Duration: ----------------------
Descent Duration: ---------------------
Total Time: ---------------------------
Total Distance Covered: ---------------
Weather Conditions:
Temperature: --------- ○ ○ ○ ○ ○ ○
Wind: ----------

(poor) (great)
Difficulty: ○ ○ ○ ○ ○ ○ ○ ○ ○
Fufillment: ○ ○ ○ ○ ○ ○ ○ ○ ○
Scenery: ○ ○ ○ ○ ○ ○ ○ ○ ○
Companions: -------------------

Notes/Photos:

Sgurr na Ruaidhe

Height: 992m
Grid Ref: NH 28902 42604

Date: ----------------------------------
Ascent Start Time: ---------------------
Descent Start Time: --------------------
Peak Time: -----------------------------
Finish Time: ---------------------------
Ascent Duration: -----------------------
Descent Duration: ----------------------
Total Time: ----------------------------
Total Distance Covered: ---------------
Weather Conditions:
Temperature: ---------
Wind: -----------

(poor) (great)
Difficulty: ○ ○ ○ ○ ○ ○ ○ ○ ○
Fufillment: ○ ○ ○ ○ ○ ○ ○ ○ ○
Scenery: ○ ○ ○ ○ ○ ○ ○ ○ ○
Companions: ----------------

Notes/Photos:

Carn nan Gobhar
Height: 992m
Grid Ref: NH 27305 43879

Date: ----------------------------
Ascent Start Time: -----------------
Descent Start Time: ----------------
Peak Time: ------------------------
Finish Time: ----------------------
Ascent Duration: ------------------
Descent Duration: -----------------
Total Time: -----------------------
Total Distance Covered: -----------
Weather Conditions:
Temperature: ---------
Wind: ----------

(poor) (great)
Difficulty: ○ ○ ○ ○ ○ ○ ○ ○ ○
Fufillment: ○ ○ ○ ○ ○ ○ ○ ○ ○
Scenery: ○ ○ ○ ○ ○ ○ ○ ○ ○
Companions: -----------------

Notes/Photos:

Carn nan Gobhar

Height: 992m
Grid Ref: NH 27305 43879

Date: ----------------------------------
Ascent Start Time: --------------------
Descent Start Time: -------------------
Peak Time: ----------------------------
Finish Time: --------------------------
Ascent Duration: ----------------------
Descent Duration: ---------------------
Total Time: ---------------------------
Total Distance Covered: ---------------
Weather Conditions: ☼ ⛅ ☁ 🌧 ⛈ ❄
Temperature: -------- ○ ○ ○ ○ ○ ○
Wind: ----------

(poor)　　　　　　　　(great)
Difficulty: ○ ○ ○ ○ ○ ○ ○ ○ ○
Fufillment: ○ ○ ○ ○ ○ ○ ○ ○ ○
Scenery: ○ ○ ○ ○ ○ ○ ○ ○ ○
Companions: ----------------

Notes/Photos:

Beinn Eighe - Spidean Coire nan Clach

Height: 993m
Grid Ref: NG 96618 59768

Date: ------------------------------
Ascent Start Time: --------------------
Descent Start Time: ------------------
Peak Time: --------------------------
Finish Time: ------------------------
Ascent Duration: --------------------
Descent Duration: -------------------
Total Time: -------------------------
Total Distance Covered: -------------
Weather Conditions:
Temperature: ---------
Wind: ----------

Difficulty: (poor) ○ ○ ○ ○ ○ ○ ○ ○ ○ ○ (great)
Fufillment: ○ ○ ○ ○ ○ ○ ○ ○ ○ ○
Scenery: ○ ○ ○ ○ ○ ○ ○ ○ ○ ○
Companions: ----------------

Notes/Photos:

Carn an Fhidhleir (Carn Ealar)

Height: 994m
Grid Ref: NN 90477 84186

Date: ----------------------------------
Ascent Start Time: ---------------------
Descent Start Time: --------------------
Peak Time: -----------------------------
Finish Time: ---------------------------
Ascent Duration: -----------------------
Descent Duration: ----------------------
Total Time: ----------------------------
Total Distance Covered: ----------------
Weather Conditions:
Temperature: _____ ○   ○   ○   ○   ○   ○
Wind: _____

(poor) (great)
Difficulty: ○ ○ ○ ○ ○ ○ ○ ○ ○ ○
Fufillment: ○ ○ ○ ○ ○ ○ ○ ○ ○ ○
Scenery: ○ ○ ○ ○ ○ ○ ○ ○ ○ ○
Companions: _____
_____
_____
_____

Notes/Photos:

Sgor na h-Ulaidh

Height: 994m
Grid Ref: NN 11121 51785

Date: ----------------------------------
Ascent Start Time: ---------------------
Descent Start Time: --------------------
Peak Time: -----------------------------
Finish Time: ---------------------------
Ascent Duration: -----------------------
Descent Duration: ----------------------
Total Time: ----------------------------
Total Distance Covered: ----------------
Weather Conditions: ☀ ⛅ ☁ 🌧 ⛈ ❄
Temperature: --------- ○ ○ ○ ○ ○ ○
Wind: ----------

(poor) (great)
Difficulty: ○ ○ ○ ○ ○ ○ ○ ○ ○
Fufillment: ○ ○ ○ ○ ○ ○ ○ ○ ○
Scenery: ○ ○ ○ ○ ○ ○ ○ ○ ○
Companions: ---------------

Notes/Photos:

An Caisteal
Height: 995m
Grid Ref: NN 37876 19336

Date: ----------------------------------

Ascent Start Time: --------------------

Descent Start Time: -------------------

Peak Time: ----------------------------

Finish Time: --------------------------

Ascent Duration: ----------------------

Descent Duration: ---------------------

Total Time: ---------------------------

Total Distance Covered: ---------------

Weather Conditions: ☀ ⛅ ☁ 🌧 ⛆ ❄

Temperature: --------- ○ ○ ○ ○ ○ ○

Wind: -----------

(poor) (great)
Difficulty: ○ ○ ○ ○ ○ ○ ○ ○ ○ ○

Fufillment: ○ ○ ○ ○ ○ ○ ○ ○ ○ ○

Scenery: ○ ○ ○ ○ ○ ○ ○ ○ ○ ○

Companions: ------------------

Notes/Photos:

Spidean Mialach

Height: 996m
Grid Ref: NH 06595 04296

Date: ....

Ascent Start Time: ....

Descent Start Time: ....

Peak Time: ....

Finish Time: ....

Ascent Duration: ....

Descent Duration: ....

Total Time: ....

Total Distance Covered: ....

Weather Conditions: ☀️ ⛅ ☁️ 🌧️ 🌦️ ❄️

Temperature: .... ○ ○ ○ ○ ○ ○

Wind: ....

(poor) (great)
Difficulty: ○ ○ ○ ○ ○ ○ ○ ○ ○ ○

Fufillment: ○ ○ ○ ○ ○ ○ ○ ○ ○ ○

Scenery: ○ ○ ○ ○ ○ ○ ○ ○ ○ ○

Companions: ....

Notes/Photos:

A'Chailleach

Height: 997m
Grid Ref: NH 13624 71401

Date: ----------------------------------

Ascent Start Time: --------------------

Descent Start Time: -------------------

Peak Time: ----------------------------

Finish Time: ---------------------------

Ascent Duration: ----------------------

Descent Duration: ---------------------

Total Time: ---------------------------

Total Distance Covered: --------------

Weather Conditions:

Temperature: _____ ○ ○ ○ ○ ○ ○

Wind: _____

(poor) (great)
Difficulty: ○ ○ ○ ○ ○ ○ ○ ○ ○

Fufillment: ○ ○ ○ ○ ○ ○ ○ ○ ○

Scenery: ○ ○ ○ ○ ○ ○ ○ ○ ○

Companions: _____

Notes/Photos:

Glas Bheinn Mhor

Height: 997m
Grid Ref: NN 15331 42973

Date: ----------------------------------

Ascent Start Time: ---------------------

Descent Start Time: --------------------

Peak Time: ----------------------------

Finish Time: --------------------------

Ascent Duration: ----------------------

Descent Duration: ---------------------

Total Time: ---------------------------

Total Distance Covered: ---------------

Weather Conditions:

Temperature: _____

Wind: _____

(poor) (great)
Difficulty: ○ ○ ○ ○ ○ ○ ○ ○ ○ ○
Fufillment: ○ ○ ○ ○ ○ ○ ○ ○ ○ ○
Scenery: ○ ○ ○ ○ ○ ○ ○ ○ ○ ○
Companions: ------------------

Notes/Photos:

Ben More Assynt

Height: 998m
Grid Ref: NC 31832 20137

Date: ---
Ascent Start Time: ---
Descent Start Time: ---
Peak Time: ---
Finish Time: ---
Ascent Duration: ---
Descent Duration: ---
Total Time: ---
Total Distance Covered: ---
Weather Conditions: ☀ ⛅ ☁ 🌧 ☔ ❄
Temperature: --- ○ ○ ○ ○ ○ ○
Wind: ---

Difficulty: (poor) ○○○○○○○○○ (great)
Fufillment: ○○○○○○○○○
Scenery: ○○○○○○○○○
Companions: ---

Notes/Photos:

Broad Cairn
Height: 998m
Grid Ref: NO 24056 81558

Date: ----------------------------------
Ascent Start Time: --------------------
Descent Start Time: -------------------
Peak Time: ----------------------------
Finish Time: ---------------------------
Ascent Duration: ----------------------
Descent Duration: ---------------------
Total Time: ---------------------------
Total Distance Covered: --------------
Weather Conditions:
Temperature: ---------
Wind: -----------

(poor) (great)
Difficulty: ○ ○ ○ ○ ○ ○ ○ ○ ○
Fufillment: ○ ○ ○ ○ ○ ○ ○ ○ ○
Scenery: ○ ○ ○ ○ ○ ○ ○ ○ ○
Companions: -------------------

Notes/Photos:

Stob Daimh [Stob Diamh]

Height: 998m
Grid Ref: NN 09486 30850

Date: ----------------------------------

Ascent Start Time: ---------------------

Descent Start Time: --------------------

Peak Time: -----------------------------

Finish Time: ---------------------------

Ascent Duration: -----------------------

Descent Duration: ----------------------

Total Time: ----------------------------

Total Distance Covered: ---------------

Weather Conditions: ☀ ⛅ ☁ 🌧 ☔ ❄

Temperature: ---------- ○ ○ ○ ○ ○ ○

Wind: ----------

(poor) (great)
Difficulty: ○ ○ ○ ○ ○ ○ ○ ○ ○ ○

Fufillment: ○ ○ ○ ○ ○ ○ ○ ○ ○ ○

Scenery: ○ ○ ○ ○ ○ ○ ○ ○ ○ ○

Companions: ----------------

Notes/Photos:

Sgurr Breac

Height: 999m
Grid Ref: NH 15843 71095

Date: ----------------------------------
Ascent Start Time: --------------------
Descent Start Time: -------------------
Peak Time: ---------------------------
Finish Time: -------------------------
Ascent Duration: ---------------------
Descent Duration: --------------------
Total Time: --------------------------
Total Distance Covered: --------------
Weather Conditions:
Temperature: ---------- ○ ○ ○ ○ ○ ○
Wind: ----------

(poor) (great)
Difficulty: ○ ○ ○ ○ ○ ○ ○ ○ ○
Fufillment: ○ ○ ○ ○ ○ ○ ○ ○ ○
Scenery: ○ ○ ○ ○ ○ ○ ○ ○ ○
Companions: -----------------

Notes/Photos:

Sgurr Choinnich

Height: 999m
Grid Ref: NH 07628 44616

Date: ----------------------------------
Ascent Start Time: --------------------
Descent Start Time: -------------------
Peak Time: ----------------------------
Finish Time: --------------------------
Ascent Duration: ----------------------
Descent Duration: ---------------------
Total Time: ---------------------------
Total Distance Covered: ---------------
Weather Conditions: ☀ ⛅ ☁ 🌧 🌦 ❄
Temperature: --------- ○ ○ ○ ○ ○ ○
Wind: -----------

(poor) (great)
Difficulty: ○ ○ ○ ○ ○ ○ ○ ○ ○
Fufillment: ○ ○ ○ ○ ○ ○ ○ ○ ○
Scenery: ○ ○ ○ ○ ○ ○ ○ ○ ○
Companions: -----------------

Notes/Photos:

Stob Ban

Height: 999m
Grid Ref: NN 14781 65434

Date: _____
Ascent Start Time: _____
Descent Start Time: _____
Peak Time: _____
Finish Time: _____
Ascent Duration: _____
Descent Duration: _____
Total Time: _____
Total Distance Covered: _____
Weather Conditions:
Temperature: _____ ○ ○ ○ ○ ○ ○
Wind: _____

(poor) (great)
Difficulty: ○ ○ ○ ○ ○ ○ ○ ○ ○ ○
Fufillment: ○ ○ ○ ○ ○ ○ ○ ○ ○ ○
Scenery: ○ ○ ○ ○ ○ ○ ○ ○ ○ ○
Companions: _____
_____
_____
_____

Notes/Photos:

Aonach Meadhoin

Height: 1001m
Grid Ref: NH 04885 13749

Date: ----------------------------------

Ascent Start Time: --------------------

Descent Start Time: -------------------

Peak Time: ------------------------------

Finish Time: ----------------------------

Ascent Duration: ------------------------

Descent Duration: -----------------------

Total Time: -----------------------------

Total Distance Covered: ----------------

Weather Conditions:

Temperature: --------- ○ ○ ○ ○ ○ ○

Wind: ----------

(poor) (great)
Difficulty: ○ ○ ○ ○ ○ ○ ○ ○ ○ ○

Fufillment: ○ ○ ○ ○ ○ ○ ○ ○ ○ ○

Scenery: ○ ○ ○ ○ ○ ○ ○ ○ ○ ○

Companions: -----------------

Notes/Photos:

Beinn a'Bheithir - Sgorr Dhonuill

Height: 1001m
Grid Ref: NN 04062 55531

Date: ....
Ascent Start Time: ....
Descent Start Time: ....
Peak Time: ....
Finish Time: ....
Ascent Duration: ....
Descent Duration: ....
Total Time: ....
Total Distance Covered: ....
Weather Conditions: ☀ ⛅ ☁ 🌧 ⛈ ❄
Temperature: .... ○ ○ ○ ○ ○ ○
Wind: ....

Difficulty: (poor) ○ ○ ○ ○ ○ ○ ○ ○ ○ (great)
Fufillment: ○ ○ ○ ○ ○ ○ ○ ○ ○
Scenery: ○ ○ ○ ○ ○ ○ ○ ○ ○
Companions: ....
....
....
....

Notes/Photos:

Meall Greigh

Height: 1001m
Grid Ref: NN 67402 43800

Date: _____

Ascent Start Time: _____

Descent Start Time: _____

Peak Time: _____

Finish Time: _____

Ascent Duration: _____

Descent Duration: _____

Total Time: _____

Total Distance Covered: _____

Weather Conditions: ☀ ⛅ ☁ 🌧 🌦 ❄

Temperature: _____ ○ ○ ○ ○ ○ ○

Wind: _____

(poor) (great)
Difficulty: ○ ○ ○ ○ ○ ○ ○ ○ ○

Fufillment: ○ ○ ○ ○ ○ ○ ○ ○ ○

Scenery: ○ ○ ○ ○ ○ ○ ○ ○ ○

Companions: _____

_____

_____

_____

Notes/Photos:

Sail Chaorainn

Height: 1002m
Grid Ref: NH 13316 15431

Date: ---------------------------------
Ascent Start Time: --------------------
Descent Start Time: -------------------
Peak Time: ----------------------------
Finish Time: --------------------------
Ascent Duration: ----------------------
Descent Duration: ---------------------
Total Time: ---------------------------
Total Distance Covered: ---------------
Weather Conditions:
Temperature: ---------- ○ ○ ○ ○ ○ ○
Wind: ----------

(poor) (great)
Difficulty: ○ ○ ○ ○ ○ ○ ○ ○ ○
Fufillment: ○ ○ ○ ○ ○ ○ ○ ○ ○
Scenery: ○ ○ ○ ○ ○ ○ ○ ○ ○
Companions: ------------------

Notes/Photos:

Sgurr na Carnach

Height: 1002m
Grid Ref: NG 97718 15880

Date: ----------------------------------
Ascent Start Time: --------------------
Descent Start Time: -------------------
Peak Time: ----------------------------
Finish Time: --------------------------
Ascent Duration: ----------------------
Descent Duration: ---------------------
Total Time: ---------------------------
Total Distance Covered: ---------------
Weather Conditions:
Temperature: ----------
Wind: ----------

Difficulty: (poor) ○ ○ ○ ○ ○ ○ ○ ○ ○ (great)
Fufillment: ○ ○ ○ ○ ○ ○ ○ ○ ○
Scenery: ○ ○ ○ ○ ○ ○ ○ ○ ○
Companions: ---------------

Notes/Photos:

Sgurr Mor

Height: 1003m
Grid Ref: NM 96539 98031

Date: ....

Ascent Start Time: ....

Descent Start Time: ....

Peak Time: ....

Finish Time: ....

Ascent Duration: ....

Descent Duration: ....

Total Time: ....

Total Distance Covered: ....

Weather Conditions:

Temperature: ....

Wind: ....

(poor) (great)
Difficulty: ○ ○ ○ ○ ○ ○ ○ ○ ○ ○

Fufillment: ○ ○ ○ ○ ○ ○ ○ ○ ○ ○

Scenery: ○ ○ ○ ○ ○ ○ ○ ○ ○ ○

Companions: ....

Notes/Photos:

Beinn an Dothaidh

Height: 1004m
Grid Ref: NN 33181 40860

Date: _____

Ascent Start Time: _____

Descent Start Time: _____

Peak Time: _____

Finish Time: _____

Ascent Duration: _____

Descent Duration: _____

Total Time: _____

Total Distance Covered: _____

Weather Conditions: ☼ ⛅ ☁ ☔ 🌬 ❄

Temperature: _____ ○ ○ ○ ○ ○ ○

Wind: _____

(poor) (great)
Difficulty: ○ ○ ○ ○ ○ ○ ○ ○ ○ ○

Fufillment: ○ ○ ○ ○ ○ ○ ○ ○ ○ ○

Scenery: ○ ○ ○ ○ ○ ○ ○ ○ ○ ○

Companions: _____

_____

_____

_____

Notes/Photos:

Sgurr an Lochain

Height: 1004m
Grid Ref: NH 00586 10417

Date: ---------------------------------
Ascent Start Time: --------------------
Descent Start Time: -------------------
Peak Time: ----------------------------
Finish Time: --------------------------
Ascent Duration: ----------------------
Descent Duration: ---------------------
Total Time: ---------------------------
Total Distance Covered: ---------------
Weather Conditions: ☀ ⛅ ☁ 🌧 ☔ ❄
Temperature: --------- ○ ○ ○ ○ ○ ○
Wind: ----------

(poor) (great)
Difficulty: ○ ○ ○ ○ ○ ○ ○ ○ ○
Fufillment: ○ ○ ○ ○ ○ ○ ○ ○ ○
Scenery: ○ ○ ○ ○ ○ ○ ○ ○ ○
Companions: -----------------

Notes/Photos:

The Devil's Point

Height: 1004m
Grid Ref: NN 97610 95106

Date: ----------------------------------
Ascent Start Time: --------------------
Descent Start Time: -------------------
Peak Time: ----------------------------
Finish Time: --------------------------
Ascent Duration: ----------------------
Descent Duration: ---------------------
Total Time: ---------------------------
Total Distance Covered: --------------
Weather Conditions: ☀ ⛅ ☁ 🌧 ⛈ ❄
Temperature: --------- ○ ○ ○ ○ ○ ○
Wind: -----------

(poor) (great)
Difficulty: ○ ○ ○ ○ ○ ○ ○ ○ ○
Fufillment: ○ ○ ○ ○ ○ ○ ○ ○ ○
Scenery: ○ ○ ○ ○ ○ ○ ○ ○ ○
Companions: -----------------

Notes/Photos:

Beinn Fhionnlaidh

Height: 1005m
Grid Ref: NH 11563 28262

Date: ----------------------------------
Ascent Start Time: ---------------------
Descent Start Time: --------------------
Peak Time: -----------------------------
Finish Time: ---------------------------
Ascent Duration: -----------------------
Descent Duration: ----------------------
Total Time: ----------------------------
Total Distance Covered: ----------------
Weather Conditions:
Temperature: ---------
Wind: ----------

(poor) (great)
Difficulty: ○ ○ ○ ○ ○ ○ ○ ○ ○ ○
Fufillment: ○ ○ ○ ○ ○ ○ ○ ○ ○ ○
Scenery: ○ ○ ○ ○ ○ ○ ○ ○ ○ ○
Companions: -------------------

Notes/Photos:

An Sgarsoch

Height: 1006m
Grid Ref: NN 93340 83676

Date: ------------------------------

Ascent Start Time: -------------------

Descent Start Time: ------------------

Peak Time: ---------------------------

Finish Time: -------------------------

Ascent Duration: ---------------------

Descent Duration: --------------------

Total Time: --------------------------

Total Distance Covered: --------------

Weather Conditions: ☀ ⛅ ☁ 🌧 ☂ ❄

Temperature: --------- ○ ○ ○ ○ ○ ○

Wind: -----------

(poor) (great)
Difficulty: ○ ○ ○ ○ ○ ○ ○ ○ ○

Fufillment: ○ ○ ○ ○ ○ ○ ○ ○ ○

Scenery: ○ ○ ○ ○ ○ ○ ○ ○ ○

Companions: ----------------

Notes/Photos:

Carn Liath

Height: 1006m
Grid Ref: NN 47231 90316

Date: ----------------------------------

Ascent Start Time: --------------------

Descent Start Time: -------------------

Peak Time: ---------------------------

Finish Time: -------------------------

Ascent Duration: ---------------------

Descent Duration: --------------------

Total Time: --------------------------

Total Distance Covered: --------------

Weather Conditions:

Temperature: ---------

Wind: -----------

(poor) (great)
Difficulty: ○ ○ ○ ○ ○ ○ ○ ○ ○

Fufillment: ○ ○ ○ ○ ○ ○ ○ ○ ○

Scenery: ○ ○ ○ ○ ○ ○ ○ ○ ○

Companions: -----------------

Notes/Photos:

Maoile Lunndaidh

Height: 1007m
Grid Ref: NH 13509 45842

Date: ....
Ascent Start Time: ....
Descent Start Time: ....
Peak Time: ....
Finish Time: ....
Ascent Duration: ....
Descent Duration: ....
Total Time: ....
Total Distance Covered: ....
Weather Conditions: ☀ ⛅ ☁ 🌧 ⛈ ❄
Temperature: .... ○ ○ ○ ○ ○ ○
Wind: ....

(poor) (great)
Difficulty: ○ ○ ○ ○ ○ ○ ○ ○ ○ ○
Fufillment: ○ ○ ○ ○ ○ ○ ○ ○ ○ ○
Scenery: ○ ○ ○ ○ ○ ○ ○ ○ ○ ○
Companions: ....
....
....
....

Notes/Photos:

Beinn Dearg

Height: 1008m
Grid Ref: NN 85297 77791

Date: ----------------------------------
Ascent Start Time: --------------------
Descent Start Time: -------------------
Peak Time: ----------------------------
Finish Time: --------------------------
Ascent Duration: ----------------------
Descent Duration: ---------------------
Total Time: ---------------------------
Total Distance Covered: ---------------
Weather Conditions:
Temperature: ----------
Wind: ----------

Difficulty: (poor) ○ ○ ○ ○ ○ ○ ○ ○ ○ (great)
Fufillment: ○ ○ ○ ○ ○ ○ ○ ○ ○
Scenery: ○ ○ ○ ○ ○ ○ ○ ○ ○
Companions: --------------------

Notes/Photos:

Beinn Udlamain
Height: 1010m
Grid Ref: NN 57947 73966

Date: ----------------------------------
Ascent Start Time: --------------------
Descent Start Time: -------------------
Peak Time: ----------------------------
Finish Time: --------------------------
Ascent Duration: ----------------------
Descent Duration: ---------------------
Total Time: ---------------------------
Total Distance Covered: ---------------
Weather Conditions: ☀ ⛅ ☁ 🌧 🌬 ❄
Temperature: --------- ○ ○ ○ ○ ○ ○
Wind: ----------

(poor) (great)
Difficulty: ○ ○ ○ ○ ○ ○ ○ ○ ○ ○
Fufillment: ○ ○ ○ ○ ○ ○ ○ ○ ○ ○
Scenery: ○ ○ ○ ○ ○ ○ ○ ○ ○ ○
Companions: ----------------

Notes/Photos:

Beinn Eighe - Ruadh-stac Mor

Height: 1010m
Grid Ref: NG 95145 61140

Date: ----------------------------------
Ascent Start Time: --------------------
Descent Start Time: -------------------
Peak Time: ----------------------------
Finish Time: --------------------------
Ascent Duration: ----------------------
Descent Duration: ---------------------
Total Time: ---------------------------
Total Distance Covered: ---------------
Weather Conditions:
Temperature: ---------
Wind: ----------

(poor) (great)
Difficulty: ○ ○ ○ ○ ○ ○ ○ ○ ○
Fufillment: ○ ○ ○ ○ ○ ○ ○ ○ ○
Scenery: ○ ○ ○ ○ ○ ○ ○ ○ ○
Companions: ----------------

Notes/Photos:

Sgurr an Doire Leathain

Height: 1010m
Grid Ref: NH 01527 09879

Date: ---------------------------------
Ascent Start Time: --------------------
Descent Start Time: -------------------
Peak Time: ----------------------------
Finish Time: --------------------------
Ascent Duration: ----------------------
Descent Duration: ---------------------
Total Time: ---------------------------
Total Distance Covered: ---------------
Weather Conditions: ☀️ ⛅ ☁️ 🌧️ 🌦️ ❄️
Temperature: _____ ○ ○ ○ ○ ○ ○
Wind: _____

(poor) (great)
Difficulty: ○ ○ ○ ○ ○ ○ ○ ○ ○ ○
Fufillment: ○ ○ ○ ○ ○ ○ ○ ○ ○ ○
Scenery: ○ ○ ○ ○ ○ ○ ○ ○ ○ ○
Companions: ------------------

Notes/Photos:

Sgurr Eilde Mor

Height: 1010m
Grid Ref: NN 23057 65779

Date: ----------------------------------

Ascent Start Time: --------------------

Descent Start Time: -------------------

Peak Time: -----------------------------

Finish Time: ---------------------------

Ascent Duration: -----------------------

Descent Duration: ----------------------

Total Time: ----------------------------

Total Distance Covered: ---------------

Weather Conditions:

Temperature: ---------

Wind: -----------

(poor) (great)
Difficulty: ○ ○ ○ ○ ○ ○ ○ ○ ○ ○

Fufillment: ○ ○ ○ ○ ○ ○ ○ ○ ○ ○

Scenery: ○ ○ ○ ○ ○ ○ ○ ○ ○ ○

Companions: --------------------

Notes/Photos:

The Saddle

Height: 1010m
Grid Ref: NG 93614 13113

Date: ----------------------------------

Ascent Start Time: --------------------

Descent Start Time: -------------------

Peak Time: -----------------------------

Finish Time: ---------------------------

Ascent Duration: -----------------------

Descent Duration: ----------------------

Total Time: ----------------------------

Total Distance Covered: ---------------

Weather Conditions:

Temperature: ---------

Wind: -----------

(poor) (great)
Difficulty: ○ ○ ○ ○ ○ ○ ○ ○ ○

Fufillment: ○ ○ ○ ○ ○ ○ ○ ○ ○

Scenery: ○ ○ ○ ○ ○ ○ ○ ○ ○

Companions: ----------------

Notes/Photos:

Beinn Ime

Height: 1011m
Grid Ref: NN 25501 08481

Date: ---------------------------------

Ascent Start Time: -------------------

Descent Start Time: ------------------

Peak Time: ---------------------------

Finish Time: -------------------------

Ascent Duration: ---------------------

Descent Duration: --------------------

Total Time: --------------------------

Total Distance Covered: --------------

Weather Conditions:

Temperature: --------- ○ ○ ○ ○ ○ ○

Wind: ----------

(poor) (great)
Difficulty: ○ ○ ○ ○ ○ ○ ○ ○ ○

Fufillment: ○ ○ ○ ○ ○ ○ ○ ○ ○

Scenery: ○ ○ ○ ○ ○ ○ ○ ○ ○

Companions: ---------------------

Notes/Photos:

Cairn Bannoch

Height: 1012m
Grid Ref: NO 22289 82546

Date: ----------------------------------

Ascent Start Time: --------------------

Descent Start Time: -------------------

Peak Time: ---------------------------

Finish Time: --------------------------

Ascent Duration: ----------------------

Descent Duration: ---------------------

Total Time: ---------------------------

Total Distance Covered: ---------------

Weather Conditions: ☀ ⛅ ☁ ☔ ☂ ❄

Temperature: --------- ○ ○ ○ ○ ○ ○

Wind: -----------

(poor) (great)
Difficulty: ○ ○ ○ ○ ○ ○ ○ ○ ○ ○

Fufillment: ○ ○ ○ ○ ○ ○ ○ ○ ○ ○

Scenery: ○ ○ ○ ○ ○ ○ ○ ○ ○ ○

Companions: ----------------

Notes/Photos:

Garbh Chioch Mhor

Height: 1013m
Grid Ref: NM 90960 96091

Date: ....

Ascent Start Time: ....

Descent Start Time: ....

Peak Time: ....

Finish Time: ....

Ascent Duration: ....

Descent Duration: ....

Total Time: ....

Total Distance Covered: ....

Weather Conditions:

Temperature: .... ○ ○ ○ ○ ○ ○

Wind: ....

(poor) (great)
Difficulty: ○ ○ ○ ○ ○ ○ ○ ○ ○

Fufillment: ○ ○ ○ ○ ○ ○ ○ ○ ○

Scenery: ○ ○ ○ ○ ○ ○ ○ ○ ○

Companions: ....

....

....

....

Notes/Photos:

Beinn Bheoil

Height: 1019m
Grid Ref: NN 51718 71713

Date: ------------------------------
Ascent Start Time: ------------------
Descent Start Time: -----------------
Peak Time: --------------------------
Finish Time: ------------------------
Ascent Duration: --------------------
Descent Duration: -------------------
Total Time: -------------------------
Total Distance Covered: -------------
Weather Conditions: ☀ ⛅ ☁ 🌧 ❄
Temperature: --------- ○ ○ ○ ○ ○ ○
Wind: ----------

(poor) (great)
Difficulty: ○ ○ ○ ○ ○ ○ ○ ○ ○
Fufillment: ○ ○ ○ ○ ○ ○ ○ ○ ○
Scenery: ○ ○ ○ ○ ○ ○ ○ ○ ○
Companions: ----------------

Notes/Photos:

Carn an Tuirc

Height: 1019m
Grid Ref: NO 17455 80473

Date: ....

Ascent Start Time: ....

Descent Start Time: ....

Peak Time: ....

Finish Time: ....

Ascent Duration: ....

Descent Duration: ....

Total Time: ....

Total Distance Covered: ....

Weather Conditions:

Temperature: ....

Wind: ....

(poor) (great)
Difficulty: ○ ○ ○ ○ ○ ○ ○ ○ ○

Fufillment: ○ ○ ○ ○ ○ ○ ○ ○ ○

Scenery: ○ ○ ○ ○ ○ ○ ○ ○ ○

Companions: ....

....

....

....

Notes/Photos:

Mullach Clach a'Bhlair

Height: 1019m
Grid Ref: NN 88286 92693

Date: ---------------------------------
Ascent Start Time: --------------------
Descent Start Time: -------------------
Peak Time: ----------------------------
Finish Time: --------------------------
Ascent Duration: ----------------------
Descent Duration: ---------------------
Total Time: ---------------------------
Total Distance Covered: ---------------
Weather Conditions:
Temperature: ○ ○ ○ ○ ○ ○
Wind: ----------

(poor) (great)
Difficulty: ○ ○ ○ ○ ○ ○ ○ ○ ○
Fufillment: ○ ○ ○ ○ ○ ○ ○ ○ ○
Scenery: ○ ○ ○ ○ ○ ○ ○ ○ ○
Companions: ---------------

Notes/Photos:

Mullach Coire Mhic Fhearchair

Height: 1019m
Grid Ref: NH 05209 73499

Date: ----------------------------------
Ascent Start Time: --------------------
Descent Start Time: -------------------
Peak Time: ----------------------------
Finish Time: --------------------------
Ascent Duration: ----------------------
Descent Duration: ---------------------
Total Time: ---------------------------
Total Distance Covered: ---------------
Weather Conditions:
Temperature: ----------
Wind: ----------

(poor) (great)
Difficulty: ○ ○ ○ ○ ○ ○ ○ ○ ○
Fufillment: ○ ○ ○ ○ ○ ○ ○ ○ ○
Scenery: ○ ○ ○ ○ ○ ○ ○ ○ ○
Companions: --------------------

Notes/Photos:

Ladhar Bheinn

Height: 1020m
Grid Ref: NG 82404 03972

Date: ----------------------------------
Ascent Start Time: ---------------------
Descent Start Time: --------------------
Peak Time: -----------------------------
Finish Time: ---------------------------
Ascent Duration: -----------------------
Descent Duration: ----------------------
Total Time: ----------------------------
Total Distance Covered: ----------------
Weather Conditions: ☀ ⛅ ☁ 🌧 ❄
Temperature: --------- ○ ○ ○ ○ ○ ○
Wind: -----------

(poor) (great)
Difficulty: ○ ○ ○ ○ ○ ○ ○ ○ ○ ○
Fufillment: ○ ○ ○ ○ ○ ○ ○ ○ ○ ○
Scenery: ○ ○ ○ ○ ○ ○ ○ ○ ○ ○
Companions: ----------------

Notes/Photos:

Buachaille Etive Mor - Stob Dearg

Height: 1021m
Grid Ref: NN 22269 54245

Date: ----------------------------------
Ascent Start Time: --------------------
Descent Start Time: -------------------
Peak Time: ----------------------------
Finish Time: --------------------------
Ascent Duration: ----------------------
Descent Duration: ---------------------
Total Time: ---------------------------
Total Distance Covered: ---------------
Weather Conditions:
Temperature: ---------- ○ ○ ○ ○ ○ ○
Wind: -----------

(poor) (great)
Difficulty: ○ ○ ○ ○ ○ ○ ○ ○ ○
Fufillment: ○ ○ ○ ○ ○ ○ ○ ○ ○
Scenery: ○ ○ ○ ○ ○ ○ ○ ○ ○
Companions: -------------------

Notes/Photos:

Aonach air Chrith

Height: 1022m
Grid Ref: NH 05106 08344

Date: ----------------------------------
Ascent Start Time: --------------------
Descent Start Time: -------------------
Peak Time: ----------------------------
Finish Time: --------------------------
Ascent Duration: ----------------------
Descent Duration: ---------------------
Total Time: ---------------------------
Total Distance Covered: ---------------
Weather Conditions: ☀ ⛅ ☁ 🌧 ☂ ❄
Temperature: --------- ○ ○ ○ ○ ○ ○
Wind: -----------

(poor) (great)
Difficulty: ○ ○ ○ ○ ○ ○ ○ ○ ○ ○
Fufillment: ○ ○ ○ ○ ○ ○ ○ ○ ○ ○
Scenery: ○ ○ ○ ○ ○ ○ ○ ○ ○ ○
Companions: ----------------

Notes/Photos:

Liathach - Mullach an Rathain

Height: 1023m
Grid Ref: NG 91191 57677

Date: ----------------------------------

Ascent Start Time: --------------------

Descent Start Time: -------------------

Peak Time: ---------------------------

Finish Time: -------------------------

Ascent Duration: ----------------------

Descent Duration: --------------------

Total Time: ---------------------------

Total Distance Covered: --------------

Weather Conditions:

Temperature: ---------

Wind: ----------

(poor) (great)
Difficulty: ○ ○ ○ ○ ○ ○ ○ ○ ○ ○

Fufillment: ○ ○ ○ ○ ○ ○ ○ ○ ○ ○

Scenery: ○ ○ ○ ○ ○ ○ ○ ○ ○ ○

Companions: ------------------

Notes/Photos:

Beinn a'Bheithir - Sgorr Dhearg

Height: 1024m
Grid Ref: NN 05688 55837

Date: ---
Ascent Start Time: ---
Descent Start Time: ---
Peak Time: ---
Finish Time: ---
Ascent Duration: ---
Descent Duration: ---
Total Time: ---
Total Distance Covered: ---
Weather Conditions:
Temperature: ---
Wind: ---

(poor) (great)
Difficulty: ○ ○ ○ ○ ○ ○ ○ ○ ○
Fufillment: ○ ○ ○ ○ ○ ○ ○ ○ ○
Scenery: ○ ○ ○ ○ ○ ○ ○ ○ ○
Companions: ---

Notes/Photos:

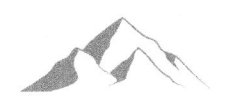

Ben Challum

Height: 1025m
Grid Ref: NN 38688 32227

Date: ----------------------------------

Ascent Start Time: --------------------

Descent Start Time: -------------------

Peak Time: ----------------------------

Finish Time: ---------------------------

Ascent Duration: ----------------------

Descent Duration: ---------------------

Total Time: ----------------------------

Total Distance Covered: --------------

Weather Conditions: ☀️ ⛅ ☁️ 🌧️ ⛈️ ❄️

Temperature: ---------- ○ ○ ○ ○ ○ ○

Wind: ----------

(poor) (great)
Difficulty: ○ ○ ○ ○ ○ ○ ○ ○ ○

Fufillment: ○ ○ ○ ○ ○ ○ ○ ○ ○

Scenery: ○ ○ ○ ○ ○ ○ ○ ○ ○

Companions: ---------------------

Notes/Photos:

Sgurr a'Mhaoraich

Height: 1027m
Grid Ref: NG 98396 06571

Date: ---
Ascent Start Time: ---
Descent Start Time: ---
Peak Time: ---
Finish Time: ---
Ascent Duration: ---
Descent Duration: ---
Total Time: ---
Total Distance Covered: ---
Weather Conditions: ☀ ⛅ ☁ 🌧 🌦 ❄
Temperature: --- ○ ○ ○ ○ ○ ○
Wind: ---

(poor) (great)
Difficulty: ○ ○ ○ ○ ○ ○ ○ ○ ○
Fufillment: ○ ○ ○ ○ ○ ○ ○ ○ ○
Scenery: ○ ○ ○ ○ ○ ○ ○ ○ ○
Companions: ---

Notes/Photos:

Sgurr na Ciste Duibhe

Height: 1027m
Grid Ref: NG 98404 14942

Date: ....

Ascent Start Time: ....

Descent Start Time: ....

Peak Time: ....

Finish Time: ....

Ascent Duration: ....

Descent Duration: ....

Total Time: ....

Total Distance Covered: ....

Weather Conditions: ☀ ⛅ ☁ 🌧 ⛈ ❄

Temperature: .... ○ ○ ○ ○ ○ ○

Wind: ....

(poor) (great)
Difficulty: ○ ○ ○ ○ ○ ○ ○ ○ ○ ○

Fufillment: ○ ○ ○ ○ ○ ○ ○ ○ ○ ○

Scenery: ○ ○ ○ ○ ○ ○ ○ ○ ○ ○

Companions: ....

....

....

....

Notes/Photos:

Ben Oss

Height: 1029m
Grid Ref: NN 28765 25340

Date: ------------------------------
Ascent Start Time: --------------------
Descent Start Time: ------------------
Peak Time: ----------------------------
Finish Time: -------------------------
Ascent Duration: ---------------------
Descent Duration: --------------------
Total Time: --------------------------
Total Distance Covered: --------------
Weather Conditions: ☀ ⛅ ☁ 🌧 🌦 ❄
Temperature: ---------- ○ ○ ○ ○ ○ ○
Wind: -----------

Difficulty: (poor) ○ ○ ○ ○ ○ ○ ○ ○ ○ ○ (great)
Fufillment: ○ ○ ○ ○ ○ ○ ○ ○ ○ ○
Scenery: ○ ○ ○ ○ ○ ○ ○ ○ ○ ○
Companions: ----------------

Notes/Photos:

Carn an Righ
Height: 1029m
Grid Ref: NO 02872 77259

Date: ----------------------------------

Ascent Start Time: --------------------

Descent Start Time: -------------------

Peak Time: ------------------------------

Finish Time: ----------------------------

Ascent Duration: ------------------------

Descent Duration: -----------------------

Total Time: -----------------------------

Total Distance Covered: ---------------

Weather Conditions:

Temperature: ---------

Wind: -----------

(poor) (great)
Difficulty: ○ ○ ○ ○ ○ ○ ○ ○ ○ ○

Fufillment: ○ ○ ○ ○ ○ ○ ○ ○ ○ ○

Scenery: ○ ○ ○ ○ ○ ○ ○ ○ ○ ○

Companions: ---------------

Notes/Photos:

Carn Gorm
Height: 1029m
Grid Ref: NN 63518 50063

Date: ....

Ascent Start Time: ....

Descent Start Time: ....

Peak Time: ....

Finish Time: ....

Ascent Duration: ....

Descent Duration: ....

Total Time: ....

Total Distance Covered: ....

Weather Conditions: ☀ ⛅ ☁ 🌧 🌬 ❄

Temperature: .... ○ ○ ○ ○ ○ ○

Wind: ....

(poor) (great)
Difficulty: ○ ○ ○ ○ ○ ○ ○ ○ ○

Fufillment: ○ ○ ○ ○ ○ ○ ○ ○ ○

Scenery: ○ ○ ○ ○ ○ ○ ○ ○ ○

Companions: ....

....

....

....

Notes/Photos:

Am Bodach

Height: 1032m
Grid Ref: NN 17641 65088

Date: _____

Ascent Start Time: _____

Descent Start Time: _____

Peak Time: _____

Finish Time: _____

Ascent Duration: _____

Descent Duration: _____

Total Time: _____

Total Distance Covered: _____

Weather Conditions: ☀ ⛅ ☁ 🌧 ⛈ ❄

Temperature: ____ ○ ○ ○ ○ ○ ○

Wind: _____

(poor) (great)
Difficulty: ○ ○ ○ ○ ○ ○ ○ ○ ○

Fufillment: ○ ○ ○ ○ ○ ○ ○ ○ ○

Scenery: ○ ○ ○ ○ ○ ○ ○ ○ ○

Companions: _____

_____

_____

_____

Notes/Photos:

Beinn Fhada

Height: 1032m
Grid Ref: NH 01859 19243

Date: ----------------------------------
Ascent Start Time: --------------------
Descent Start Time: -------------------
Peak Time: ----------------------------
Finish Time: --------------------------
Ascent Duration: ----------------------
Descent Duration: ---------------------
Total Time: ---------------------------
Total Distance Covered: ---------------
Weather Conditions: ☼ ⛅ ☁ 🌧 ⛆ ❄
Temperature: ------- ○ ○ ○ ○ ○ ○
Wind: -----------

Difficulty: (poor) ○ ○ ○ ○ ○ ○ ○ ○ ○ ○ (great)
Fufillment: ○ ○ ○ ○ ○ ○ ○ ○ ○ ○
Scenery: ○ ○ ○ ○ ○ ○ ○ ○ ○ ○
Companions: -----------------

Notes/Photos:

Carn Dearg

Height: 1034m
Grid Ref: NN 50419 76435

Date: _____

Ascent Start Time: _____

Descent Start Time: _____

Peak Time: _____

Finish Time: _____

Ascent Duration: _____

Descent Duration: _____

Total Time: _____

Total Distance Covered: _____

Weather Conditions:

Temperature: _____ ○ ○ ○ ○ ○ ○

Wind: _____

(poor) (great)
Difficulty: ○ ○ ○ ○ ○ ○ ○ ○ ○

Fufillment: ○ ○ ○ ○ ○ ○ ○ ○ ○

Scenery: ○ ○ ○ ○ ○ ○ ○ ○ ○

Companions: _____

_____

_____

_____

Notes/Photos:

Gleouraich

Height: 1035m
Grid Ref: NH 03948 05335

Date: ---------------------------------
Ascent Start Time: --------------------
Descent Start Time: -------------------
Peak Time: ---------------------------
Finish Time: -------------------------
Ascent Duration: ---------------------
Descent Duration: --------------------
Total Time: --------------------------
Total Distance Covered: --------------
Weather Conditions: ☀ ⛅ ☁ 🌧 ❄
Temperature: _____ ○ ○ ○ ○ ○ ○
Wind: _____

(poor) (great)
Difficulty: ○ ○ ○ ○ ○ ○ ○ ○ ○
Fufillment: ○ ○ ○ ○ ○ ○ ○ ○ ○
Scenery: ○ ○ ○ ○ ○ ○ ○ ○ ○
Companions: _____
_____
_____
_____

Notes/Photos:

Sgurr a'Bhealaich Dheirg

Height: 1036m
Grid Ref: NH 03520 14349

Date: ----------------------------------
Ascent Start Time: ---------------------
Descent Start Time: --------------------
Peak Time: -----------------------------
Finish Time: ---------------------------
Ascent Duration: -----------------------
Descent Duration: ----------------------
Total Time: ----------------------------
Total Distance Covered: ----------------
Weather Conditions: ☀ ⛅ ☁ 🌧 ⛈ ❄
Temperature: --------- ○ ○ ○ ○ ○ ○
Wind: ----------

(poor)　　　　　　　　　(great)
Difficulty: ○ ○ ○ ○ ○ ○ ○ ○ ○
Fufillment: ○ ○ ○ ○ ○ ○ ○ ○ ○
Scenery: ○ ○ ○ ○ ○ ○ ○ ○ ○
Companions: ----------------

Notes/Photos:

Carn a'Mhaim

Height: 1037m
Grid Ref: NN 99459 95190

Date: ----------------------------------
Ascent Start Time: --------------------
Descent Start Time: -------------------
Peak Time: ----------------------------
Finish Time: --------------------------
Ascent Duration: ----------------------
Descent Duration: ---------------------
Total Time: ---------------------------
Total Distance Covered: ---------------
Weather Conditions:
Temperature: ---------
Wind: ----------

(poor) (great)
Difficulty: ○ ○ ○ ○ ○ ○ ○ ○ ○ ○
Fufillment: ○ ○ ○ ○ ○ ○ ○ ○ ○ ○
Scenery: ○ ○ ○ ○ ○ ○ ○ ○ ○ ○
Companions: ---------------

Notes/Photos:

Beinn Achaladair

Height: 1038m
Grid Ref: NN 34471 43234

Date: ....

Ascent Start Time: ....

Descent Start Time: ....

Peak Time: ....

Finish Time: ....

Ascent Duration: ....

Descent Duration: ....

Total Time: ....

Total Distance Covered: ....

Weather Conditions:

Temperature: ....

Wind: ....

(poor) (great)
Difficulty: ○ ○ ○ ○ ○ ○ ○ ○ ○

Fufillment: ○ ○ ○ ○ ○ ○ ○ ○ ○

Scenery: ○ ○ ○ ○ ○ ○ ○ ○ ○

Companions: ....

....

....

....

Notes/Photos:

Meall Ghaordaidh

Height: 1039m
Grid Ref: NN 51445 39696

Date: ------------------------------------
Ascent Start Time: ---------------------
Descent Start Time: --------------------
Peak Time: -----------------------------
Finish Time: ----------------------------
Ascent Duration: -----------------------
Descent Duration: ---------------------
Total Time: -----------------------------
Total Distance Covered: ---------------
Weather Conditions:
Temperature: ○ ○ ○ ○ ○ ○
Wind: -----------

(poor) (great)
Difficulty: ○ ○ ○ ○ ○ ○ ○ ○ ○
Fufillment: ○ ○ ○ ○ ○ ○ ○ ○ ○
Scenery: ○ ○ ○ ○ ○ ○ ○ ○ ○
Companions: ------------------

Notes/Photos:

Sgurr na Ciche

Height: 1040m
Grid Ref: NM 90224 96676

Date: ----------------------------------
Ascent Start Time: --------------------
Descent Start Time: -------------------
Peak Time: ----------------------------
Finish Time: --------------------------
Ascent Duration: ----------------------
Descent Duration: ---------------------
Total Time: ---------------------------
Total Distance Covered: ---------------
Weather Conditions:
Temperature: ---------
Wind: ----------

(poor) (great)
Difficulty: ○ ○ ○ ○ ○ ○ ○ ○ ○
Fufillment: ○ ○ ○ ○ ○ ○ ○ ○ ○
Scenery: ○ ○ ○ ○ ○ ○ ○ ○ ○
Companions: ----------------

Notes/Photos:

Carn Mairg

Height: 1042m
Grid Ref: NN 68493 51252

Date:
Ascent Start Time:
Descent Start Time:
Peak Time:
Finish Time:
Ascent Duration:
Descent Duration:
Total Time:
Total Distance Covered:
Weather Conditions: ☀ ⛅ ☁ 🌧 🌦 ❄
Temperature: ○ ○ ○ ○ ○ ○
Wind:

(poor) (great)
Difficulty: ○ ○ ○ ○ ○ ○ ○ ○ ○
Fufillment: ○ ○ ○ ○ ○ ○ ○ ○ ○
Scenery: ○ ○ ○ ○ ○ ○ ○ ○ ○
Companions:

Notes/Photos:

Meall nan Tarmachan

Height: 1044m
Grid Ref: NN 58521 38990

Date: ----------------------------------
Ascent Start Time: --------------------
Descent Start Time: -------------------
Peak Time: ----------------------------
Finish Time: --------------------------
Ascent Duration: ----------------------
Descent Duration: ---------------------
Total Time: ---------------------------
Total Distance Covered: ---------------
Weather Conditions:
Temperature: -----------
Wind: ----------

(poor) (great)
Difficulty: ○ ○ ○ ○ ○ ○ ○ ○ ○ ○
Fufillment: ○ ○ ○ ○ ○ ○ ○ ○ ○ ○
Scenery: ○ ○ ○ ○ ○ ○ ○ ○ ○ ○
Companions: -------------------

Notes/Photos:

Stob Coir' an Albannaich

Height: 1044m
Grid Ref: NN 16956 44294

Date: ----------------------------------

Ascent Start Time: --------------------

Descent Start Time: -------------------

Peak Time: ---------------------------

Finish Time: --------------------------

Ascent Duration: ---------------------

Descent Duration: --------------------

Total Time: ---------------------------

Total Distance Covered: --------------

Weather Conditions:

Temperature: --------- ○ ○ ○ ○ ○ ○

Wind: -----------

(poor) (great)
Difficulty: ○ ○ ○ ○ ○ ○ ○ ○ ○

Fufillment: ○ ○ ○ ○ ○ ○ ○ ○ ○

Scenery: ○ ○ ○ ○ ○ ○ ○ ○ ○

Companions: ---------------

Notes/Photos:

Beinn Iutharn Mhor

Height: 1045m
Grid Ref: NO 04567 79270

Date: _____
Ascent Start Time: _____
Descent Start Time: _____
Peak Time: _____
Finish Time: _____
Ascent Duration: _____
Descent Duration: _____
Total Time: _____
Total Distance Covered: _____
Weather Conditions:
Temperature: _____
Wind: _____

(poor) (great)
Difficulty: ○ ○ ○ ○ ○ ○ ○ ○ ○
Fufillment: ○ ○ ○ ○ ○ ○ ○ ○ ○
Scenery: ○ ○ ○ ○ ○ ○ ○ ○ ○
Companions: _____
_____
_____
_____

Notes/Photos:

Ben Wyvis - Glas Leathad Mor

Height: 1046m
Grid Ref: NH 46299 68368

Date: ----------------------------------

Ascent Start Time: ---------------------

Descent Start Time: --------------------

Peak Time: ----------------------------

Finish Time: ---------------------------

Ascent Duration: -----------------------

Descent Duration: ----------------------

Total Time: ----------------------------

Total Distance Covered: ---------------

Weather Conditions: ☀ ⛅ ☁ 🌧 ❄ ❋

Temperature: -------- ○ ○ ○ ○ ○ ○

Wind: ----------

(poor) (great)
Difficulty: ○ ○ ○ ○ ○ ○ ○ ○ ○

Fufillment: ○ ○ ○ ○ ○ ○ ○ ○ ○

Scenery: ○ ○ ○ ○ ○ ○ ○ ○ ○

Companions: ----------------

Notes/Photos:

Chno Dearg

Height: 1046m
Grid Ref: NN 37744 74106

Date: ----------------------------

Ascent Start Time: -------------------

Descent Start Time: ------------------

Peak Time: ---------------------------

Finish Time: --------------------------

Ascent Duration: ----------------------

Descent Duration: ---------------------

Total Time: ----------------------------

Total Distance Covered: --------------

Weather Conditions:

Temperature: --------- ○ ○ ○ ○ ○ ○

Wind: ----------

(poor) (great)
Difficulty: ○ ○ ○ ○ ○ ○ ○ ○ ○

Fufillment: ○ ○ ○ ○ ○ ○ ○ ○ ○

Scenery: ○ ○ ○ ○ ○ ○ ○ ○ ○

Companions: -------------------

Notes/Photos:

Cruach Ardrain

Height: 1046m
Grid Ref: NN 40930 21207

Date: ....
Ascent Start Time: ....
Descent Start Time: ....
Peak Time: ....
Finish Time: ....
Ascent Duration: ....
Descent Duration: ....
Total Time: ....
Total Distance Covered: ....
Weather Conditions: ☀ ⛅ ☁ 🌧 🌦 ❄
Temperature: .... ○ ○ ○ ○ ○ ○
Wind: ....

(poor)   (great)
Difficulty: ○ ○ ○ ○ ○ ○ ○ ○ ○
Fufillment: ○ ○ ○ ○ ○ ○ ○ ○ ○
Scenery: ○ ○ ○ ○ ○ ○ ○ ○ ○
Companions: ....
....
....
....

Notes/Photos:

Carn an t-Sagairt Mor

Height: 1047m
Grid Ref: NO 20811 84271

Date: ----------------------------------

Ascent Start Time: --------------------

Descent Start Time: -------------------

Peak Time: -----------------------------

Finish Time: ---------------------------

Ascent Duration: -----------------------

Descent Duration: ----------------------

Total Time: -----------------------------

Total Distance Covered: ---------------

Weather Conditions:

Temperature: ---------

Wind: -----------

(poor) (great)
Difficulty: ○ ○ ○ ○ ○ ○ ○ ○ ○ ○

Fufillment: ○ ○ ○ ○ ○ ○ ○ ○ ○ ○

Scenery: ○ ○ ○ ○ ○ ○ ○ ○ ○ ○

Companions: --------------------

Notes/Photos:

Creag Mhor

Height: 1047m
Grid Ref: NN 39153 36103

Date: ----------------------------------

Ascent Start Time: ---------------------

Descent Start Time: --------------------

Peak Time: ------------------------------

Finish Time: ----------------------------

Ascent Duration: ------------------------

Descent Duration: -----------------------

Total Time: -----------------------------

Total Distance Covered: -----------------

Weather Conditions:

Temperature: ---------

Wind: ----------

(poor) (great)
Difficulty: ○ ○ ○ ○ ○ ○ ○ ○ ○ ○

Fufillment: ○ ○ ○ ○ ○ ○ ○ ○ ○ ○

Scenery: ○ ○ ○ ○ ○ ○ ○ ○ ○ ○

Companions: -----------------

Notes/Photos:

Geal Charn

Height: 1049m
Grid Ref: NN 50434 81172

Date: ------------------------------
Ascent Start Time: -------------------
Descent Start Time: ------------------
Peak Time: ---------------------------
Finish Time: -------------------------
Ascent Duration: ---------------------
Descent Duration: --------------------
Total Time: --------------------------
Total Distance Covered: --------------
Weather Conditions: ☀ ⛅ ☁ 🌧 ⛈ ❄
Temperature: --------- ○ ○ ○ ○ ○ ○
Wind: ----------

(poor) (great)
Difficulty: ○ ○ ○ ○ ○ ○ ○ ○ ○
Fufillment: ○ ○ ○ ○ ○ ○ ○ ○ ○
Scenery: ○ ○ ○ ○ ○ ○ ○ ○ ○
Companions: ------------------

Notes/Photos:

Sgurr Fhuar-thuill

Height: 1049m
Grid Ref: NH 23583 43743

Date: ----------------------------------
Ascent Start Time: --------------------
Descent Start Time: -------------------
Peak Time: ----------------------------
Finish Time: --------------------------
Ascent Duration: ----------------------
Descent Duration: ---------------------
Total Time: ---------------------------
Total Distance Covered: ---------------
Weather Conditions: ☀ ⛅ ☁ 🌧 🌦 ❄
Temperature: -------- ○ ○ ○ ○ ○ ○
Wind: ----------

(poor) (great)
Difficulty: ○ ○ ○ ○ ○ ○ ○ ○ ○
Fufillment: ○ ○ ○ ○ ○ ○ ○ ○ ○
Scenery: ○ ○ ○ ○ ○ ○ ○ ○ ○
Companions: ---------------

Notes/Photos:

Beinn a'Chaorainn

Height: 1050m
Grid Ref: NN 38608 85053

Date: ....
Ascent Start Time: ....
Descent Start Time: ....
Peak Time: ....
Finish Time: ....
Ascent Duration: ....
Descent Duration: ....
Total Time: ....
Total Distance Covered: ....
Weather Conditions:
Temperature: ....
Wind: ....

Difficulty: (poor) ○ ○ ○ ○ ○ ○ ○ ○ ○ ○ (great)
Fufillment: ○ ○ ○ ○ ○ ○ ○ ○ ○ ○
Scenery: ○ ○ ○ ○ ○ ○ ○ ○ ○ ○
Companions: ....
....
....
....

Notes/Photos:

Glas Tulaichean

Height: 1051m
Grid Ref: NO 05106 76002

Date: ----------------------------------
Ascent Start Time: --------------------
Descent Start Time: -------------------
Peak Time: ----------------------------
Finish Time: --------------------------
Ascent Duration: ----------------------
Descent Duration: ---------------------
Total Time: ---------------------------
Total Distance Covered: ---------------
Weather Conditions: ☀ ⛅ ☁ 🌧 ⛈ ❄
Temperature: --------- ○ ○ ○ ○ ○ ○
Wind: ----------

(poor)   (great)
Difficulty: ○ ○ ○ ○ ○ ○ ○ ○ ○
Fufillment: ○ ○ ○ ○ ○ ○ ○ ○ ○
Scenery: ○ ○ ○ ○ ○ ○ ○ ○ ○
Companions: ------------------

Notes/Photos:

Sgurr a'Chaorachain

Height: 1053m
Grid Ref: NH 08752 44727

Date: ----------------------------------
Ascent Start Time: --------------------
Descent Start Time: -------------------
Peak Time: ---------------------------
Finish Time: --------------------------
Ascent Duration: ----------------------
Descent Duration: ---------------------
Total Time: ---------------------------
Total Distance Covered: ---------------
Weather Conditions: ☀ ⛅ ☁ 🌧 💨 ❄
Temperature: --------- ○ ○ ○ ○ ○ ○
Wind: ----------

Difficulty: (poor) ○ ○ ○ ○ ○ ○ ○ ○ ○ ○ (great)
Fufillment: ○ ○ ○ ○ ○ ○ ○ ○ ○ ○
Scenery: ○ ○ ○ ○ ○ ○ ○ ○ ○ ○
Companions: ----------------

Notes/Photos:

Stob Poite Coire Ardair

Height: 1054m
Grid Ref: NN 42887 88835

Date: ----------------------------------
Ascent Start Time: ---------------------
Descent Start Time: --------------------
Peak Time: -----------------------------
Finish Time: ---------------------------
Ascent Duration: -----------------------
Descent Duration: ----------------------
Total Time: ----------------------------
Total Distance Covered: ----------------
Weather Conditions:
Temperature: ---------- ○ ○ ○ ○ ○ ○
Wind: -----------

(poor) (great)
Difficulty: ○ ○ ○ ○ ○ ○ ○ ○ ○ ○
Fufillment: ○ ○ ○ ○ ○ ○ ○ ○ ○ ○
Scenery: ○ ○ ○ ○ ○ ○ ○ ○ ○ ○
Companions: ----------------

Notes/Photos:

Toll Creagach
Height: 1054m
Grid Ref: NH 19404 28269

Date: ------------------------------

Ascent Start Time: -------------------

Descent Start Time: ------------------

Peak Time: ---------------------------

Finish Time: -------------------------

Ascent Duration: ---------------------

Descent Duration: --------------------

Total Time: --------------------------

Total Distance Covered: --------------

Weather Conditions:

Temperature: ---------

Wind: ----------

(poor) (great)
Difficulty: ○ ○ ○ ○ ○ ○ ○ ○ ○

Fufillment: ○ ○ ○ ○ ○ ○ ○ ○ ○

Scenery: ○ ○ ○ ○ ○ ○ ○ ○ ○

Companions: -------------------

Notes/Photos:

Liathach - Spidean a'Choire Leith

Height: 1055m
Grid Ref: NG 92937 57957

Date: ....
Ascent Start Time: ....
Descent Start Time: ....
Peak Time: ....
Finish Time: ....
Ascent Duration: ....
Descent Duration: ....
Total Time: ....
Total Distance Covered: ....
Weather Conditions: ☼ ⛅ ☁ 🌧 🌦 ❄
Temperature: .... ○ ○ ○ ○ ○ ○
Wind: ....

(poor) (great)
Difficulty: ○ ○ ○ ○ ○ ○ ○ ○ ○ ○
Fufillment: ○ ○ ○ ○ ○ ○ ○ ○ ○ ○
Scenery: ○ ○ ○ ○ ○ ○ ○ ○ ○ ○
Companions: ....
....
....
....

Notes/Photos:

Na Gruagaichean

Height: 1056m
Grid Ref: NN 20310 65191

Date: ---------------------------------
Ascent Start Time: --------------------
Descent Start Time: -------------------
Peak Time: ---------------------------
Finish Time: -------------------------
Ascent Duration: ---------------------
Descent Duration: --------------------
Total Time: --------------------------
Total Distance Covered: --------------
Weather Conditions: ☀ ⛅ ☁ 🌧 ⛈ ❄
Temperature: --------- ○ ○ ○ ○ ○ ○
Wind: ----------

(poor) (great)
Difficulty: ○ ○ ○ ○ ○ ○ ○ ○ ○
Fufillment: ○ ○ ○ ○ ○ ○ ○ ○ ○
Scenery: ○ ○ ○ ○ ○ ○ ○ ○ ○
Companions: ------------------

Notes/Photos:

An Teallach - Sgurr Fiona

Height: 1060m
Grid Ref: NH 06409 83667

Date: ----------------------------------
Ascent Start Time: --------------------
Descent Start Time: -------------------
Peak Time: ----------------------------
Finish Time: --------------------------
Ascent Duration: ----------------------
Descent Duration: ---------------------
Total Time: ---------------------------
Total Distance Covered: ---------------
Weather Conditions:
Temperature: _____ ○ ○ ○ ○ ○ ○
Wind: ----------

(poor) (great)
Difficulty: ○ ○ ○ ○ ○ ○ ○ ○ ○
Fufillment: ○ ○ ○ ○ ○ ○ ○ ○ ○
Scenery: ○ ○ ○ ○ ○ ○ ○ ○ ○
Companions: ---------------

Notes/Photos:

An Teallach - Bidein a'Ghlas Thuill
Height: 1062m
Grid Ref: NH 06899 84354

Date: ----------------------------------

Ascent Start Time: --------------------

Descent Start Time: -------------------

Peak Time: ----------------------------

Finish Time: --------------------------

Ascent Duration: ----------------------

Descent Duration: ---------------------

Total Time: ---------------------------

Total Distance Covered: ---------------

Weather Conditions:

Temperature: ----------

Wind: -----------

(poor) (great)
Difficulty: ○ ○ ○ ○ ○ ○ ○ ○ ○ ○

Fufillment: ○ ○ ○ ○ ○ ○ ○ ○ ○ ○

Scenery: ○ ○ ○ ○ ○ ○ ○ ○ ○ ○

Companions: ---------------

Notes/Photos:

Cairn of Claise

Height: 1064m
Grid Ref: NO 18550 78881

Date: ------------------------------

Ascent Start Time: --------------------

Descent Start Time: -------------------

Peak Time: ----------------------------

Finish Time: --------------------------

Ascent Duration: ----------------------

Descent Duration: ---------------------

Total Time: ---------------------------

Total Distance Covered: ---------------

Weather Conditions: ☀ ⛅ ☁ 🌧 🌬 ❄

Temperature: -------- ○ ○ ○ ○ ○ ○

Wind: -----------

(poor) (great)
Difficulty: ○ ○ ○ ○ ○ ○ ○ ○ ○

Fufillment: ○ ○ ○ ○ ○ ○ ○ ○ ○

Scenery: ○ ○ ○ ○ ○ ○ ○ ○ ○

Companions: ---------------

Notes/Photos:

Sgurr Fhuaran

Height: 1067m
Grid Ref: NG 97852 16667

Date: _____

Ascent Start Time: _____

Descent Start Time: _____

Peak Time: _____

Finish Time: _____

Ascent Duration: _____

Descent Duration: _____

Total Time: _____

Total Distance Covered: _____

Weather Conditions: ☀ ⛅ ☁ 🌧 ⛈ ❄

Temperature: _____ ○ ○ ○ ○ ○ ○

Wind: _____

(poor) (great)
Difficulty: ○ ○ ○ ○ ○ ○ ○ ○ ○

Fufillment: ○ ○ ○ ○ ○ ○ ○ ○ ○

Scenery: ○ ○ ○ ○ ○ ○ ○ ○ ○

Companions: _____

_____

_____

_____

Notes/Photos:

Glas Maol

Height: 1068m
Grid Ref: NO 16700 76567

Date: ----------------------------------
Ascent Start Time: --------------------
Descent Start Time: -------------------
Peak Time: ---------------------------
Finish Time: --------------------------
Ascent Duration: ----------------------
Descent Duration: ---------------------
Total Time: ---------------------------
Total Distance Covered: ---------------
Weather Conditions:
Temperature: ---------
Wind: ----------

(poor) (great)
Difficulty: ○ ○ ○ ○ ○ ○ ○ ○ ○
Fufillment: ○ ○ ○ ○ ○ ○ ○ ○ ○
Scenery: ○ ○ ○ ○ ○ ○ ○ ○ ○
Companions: ------------------

Notes/Photos:

An Socach

Height: 1069m
Grid Ref: NH 10064 33263

Date: ----------------------------------

Ascent Start Time: --------------------

Descent Start Time: -------------------

Peak Time: ----------------------------

Finish Time: --------------------------

Ascent Duration: ----------------------

Descent Duration: ---------------------

Total Time: ---------------------------

Total Distance Covered: ---------------

Weather Conditions: ☀ ⛅ ☁ 🌧 ⛈ ❄

Temperature: --------- ○ ○ ○ ○ ○ ○

Wind: -----------

(poor) (great)
Difficulty: ○ ○ ○ ○ ○ ○ ○ ○ ○

Fufillment: ○ ○ ○ ○ ○ ○ ○ ○ ○

Scenery: ○ ○ ○ ○ ○ ○ ○ ○ ○

Companions: -----------------

Notes/Photos:

Meall Corranaich

Height: 1069m
Grid Ref: NN 61536 41039

Date: ----------------------------------

Ascent Start Time: --------------------

Descent Start Time: -------------------

Peak Time: ----------------------------

Finish Time: --------------------------

Ascent Duration: ----------------------

Descent Duration: ---------------------

Total Time: ---------------------------

Total Distance Covered: ---------------

Weather Conditions:

Temperature: ⚬ ⚬ ⚬ ⚬ ⚬ ⚬

Wind: ----------

(poor) (great)
Difficulty: ⚬ ⚬ ⚬ ⚬ ⚬ ⚬ ⚬ ⚬ ⚬ ⚬

Fufillment: ⚬ ⚬ ⚬ ⚬ ⚬ ⚬ ⚬ ⚬ ⚬ ⚬

Scenery: ⚬ ⚬ ⚬ ⚬ ⚬ ⚬ ⚬ ⚬ ⚬ ⚬

Companions: ------------------

Notes/Photos:

Beinn a'Ghlo

Height: 1070m
Grid Ref: NN 94564 72394

Date: ----------------------------------
Ascent Start Time: --------------------
Descent Start Time: -------------------
Peak Time: ----------------------------
Finish Time: --------------------------
Ascent Duration: ----------------------
Descent Duration: ---------------------
Total Time: ---------------------------
Total Distance Covered: ---------------
Weather Conditions:
Temperature: ---------
Wind: -----------

(poor) (great)
Difficulty: ○ ○ ○ ○ ○ ○ ○ ○ ○ ○
Fufillment: ○ ○ ○ ○ ○ ○ ○ ○ ○ ○
Scenery: ○ ○ ○ ○ ○ ○ ○ ○ ○ ○
Companions: ---------------

Notes/Photos:

Stob Coire Sgreamhach

Height: 1072m
Grid Ref: NN 15491 53655

Date: ----------------------------------

Ascent Start Time: ---------------------

Descent Start Time: --------------------

Peak Time: -----------------------------

Finish Time: ---------------------------

Ascent Duration: -----------------------

Descent Duration: ----------------------

Total Time: ----------------------------

Total Distance Covered: ----------------

Weather Conditions:

Temperature: ----------

Wind: -----------

(poor) (great)
Difficulty: ○ ○ ○ ○ ○ ○ ○ ○ ○ ○

Fufillment: ○ ○ ○ ○ ○ ○ ○ ○ ○ ○

Scenery: ○ ○ ○ ○ ○ ○ ○ ○ ○ ○

Companions: ----------------

Notes/Photos:

Beinn Dorain
Height: 1076m
Grid Ref: NN 32557 37847

Date: _____
Ascent Start Time: _____
Descent Start Time: _____
Peak Time: _____
Finish Time: _____
Ascent Duration: _____
Descent Duration: _____
Total Time: _____
Total Distance Covered: _____
Weather Conditions:
Temperature: _____
Wind: _____

Difficulty: (poor) ○ ○ ○ ○ ○ ○ ○ ○ ○ (great)
Fufillment: ○ ○ ○ ○ ○ ○ ○ ○ ○
Scenery: ○ ○ ○ ○ ○ ○ ○ ○ ○
Companions: _____
_____
_____
_____

Notes/Photos:

Beinn Heasgarnich

Height: 1078m
Grid Ref: NN 41383 38331

Date: ----------------------------------

Ascent Start Time: ---------------------

Descent Start Time: -------------------

Peak Time: ----------------------------

Finish Time: --------------------------

Ascent Duration: ----------------------

Descent Duration: ---------------------

Total Time: ---------------------------

Total Distance Covered: ---------------

Weather Conditions:

Temperature: ---------

Wind: -----------

(poor) (great)
Difficulty: ○ ○ ○ ○ ○ ○ ○ ○ ○

Fufillment: ○ ○ ○ ○ ○ ○ ○ ○ ○

Scenery: ○ ○ ○ ○ ○ ○ ○ ○ ○

Companions: ---------------

Notes/Photos:

Ben Starav

Height: 1078m
Grid Ref: NN 12580 42705

Date: ----------------------------------
Ascent Start Time: --------------------
Descent Start Time: -------------------
Peak Time: ----------------------------
Finish Time: --------------------------
Ascent Duration: ----------------------
Descent Duration: ---------------------
Total Time: ---------------------------
Total Distance Covered: ---------------
Weather Conditions:
Temperature: --------- ○ ○ ○ ○ ○ ○
Wind: -----------

(poor) (great)
Difficulty: ○ ○ ○ ○ ○ ○ ○ ○ ○
Fufillment: ○ ○ ○ ○ ○ ○ ○ ○ ○
Scenery: ○ ○ ○ ○ ○ ○ ○ ○ ○
Companions: --------------------

Notes/Photos:

Beinn a'Chreachain

Height: 1081m
Grid Ref: NN 37390 44067

Date: ----------------------------------

Ascent Start Time: --------------------

Descent Start Time: -------------------

Peak Time: ----------------------------

Finish Time: --------------------------

Ascent Duration: ----------------------

Descent Duration: ---------------------

Total Time: ---------------------------

Total Distance Covered: ---------------

Weather Conditions:

Temperature: ---------

Wind: -----------

(poor) (great)
Difficulty: ○ ○ ○ ○ ○ ○ ○ ○ ○

Fufillment: ○ ○ ○ ○ ○ ○ ○ ○ ○

Scenery: ○ ○ ○ ○ ○ ○ ○ ○ ○

Companions: ------------------

Notes/Photos:

Beinn a'Chaorainn

Height: 1082m
Grid Ref: NJ 04516 01351

Date: ----------------------------------
Ascent Start Time: --------------------
Descent Start Time: ------------------
Peak Time: -----------------------------
Finish Time: ---------------------------
Ascent Duration: ---------------------
Descent Duration: --------------------
Total Time: ----------------------------
Total Distance Covered: --------------
Weather Conditions: ☀ ⛅ ☁ 🌧 ⛆ ❄
Temperature: --------- ○ ○ ○ ○ ○ ○
Wind: -----------

(poor) (great)
Difficulty: ○ ○ ○ ○ ○ ○ ○ ○ ○ ○
Fufillment: ○ ○ ○ ○ ○ ○ ○ ○ ○ ○
Scenery: ○ ○ ○ ○ ○ ○ ○ ○ ○ ○
Companions: ----------------

Notes/Photos:

Schiehallion

Height: 1083m
Grid Ref: NN 71386 54760

Date: ----------------------------------

Ascent Start Time: ---------------------

Descent Start Time: -------------------

Peak Time: -----------------------------

Finish Time: ---------------------------

Ascent Duration: -----------------------

Descent Duration: ----------------------

Total Time: ----------------------------

Total Distance Covered: ---------------

Weather Conditions: ☀ ⛅ ☁ 🌧 🌦 ❄

Temperature: ------- ○ ○ ○ ○ ○ ○

Wind: ----------

(poor) (great)
Difficulty: ○ ○ ○ ○ ○ ○ ○ ○ ○ ○

Fufillment: ○ ○ ○ ○ ○ ○ ○ ○ ○ ○

Scenery: ○ ○ ○ ○ ○ ○ ○ ○ ○ ○

Companions: ---------------

Notes/Photos:

Sgurr a'Choire Ghlais

Height: 1083m
Grid Ref: NH 25838 43045

Date: _____
Ascent Start Time: _____
Descent Start Time: _____
Peak Time: _____
Finish Time: _____
Ascent Duration: _____
Descent Duration: _____
Total Time: _____
Total Distance Covered: _____
Weather Conditions: ☀ ⛅ ☁ 🌧 ⛈ ❄
Temperature: _____ ○ ○ ○ ○ ○ ○
Wind: _____

(poor) (great)
Difficulty: ○ ○ ○ ○ ○ ○ ○ ○ ○
Fufillment: ○ ○ ○ ○ ○ ○ ○ ○ ○
Scenery: ○ ○ ○ ○ ○ ○ ○ ○ ○
Companions: _____
_____
_____
_____

Notes/Photos:

Beinn Dearg

Height: 1084m
Grid Ref: NH 25935 81171

Date: ---------------------------------
Ascent Start Time: --------------------
Descent Start Time: -------------------
Peak Time: ----------------------------
Finish Time: --------------------------
Ascent Duration: ----------------------
Descent Duration: ---------------------
Total Time: ---------------------------
Total Distance Covered: --------------
Weather Conditions: ☀ ⛅ ☁ 🌧 🌬 ❄
Temperature: --------- ○ ○ ○ ○ ○ ○
Wind: -----------

(poor) (great)
Difficulty: ○ ○ ○ ○ ○ ○ ○ ○ ○
Fufillment: ○ ○ ○ ○ ○ ○ ○ ○ ○
Scenery: ○ ○ ○ ○ ○ ○ ○ ○ ○
Companions: ------------------

Notes/Photos:

Beinn a'Chlachair

Height: 1087m
Grid Ref: NN 47125 78146

Date: _____

Ascent Start Time: _____

Descent Start Time: _____

Peak Time: _____

Finish Time: _____

Ascent Duration: _____

Descent Duration: _____

Total Time: _____

Total Distance Covered: _____

Weather Conditions: ☀ ⛅ ☁ 🌧 🌦 ❄

Temperature: _____ ○ ○ ○ ○ ○ ○

Wind: _____

(poor) (great)
Difficulty: ○ ○ ○ ○ ○ ○ ○ ○ ○

Fufillment: ○ ○ ○ ○ ○ ○ ○ ○ ○

Scenery: ○ ○ ○ ○ ○ ○ ○ ○ ○

Companions: _____

_____

_____

_____

Notes/Photos:

Bynack More

Height: 1090m
Grid Ref: NJ 04191 06364

Date: ----------------------------------

Ascent Start Time: --------------------

Descent Start Time: -------------------

Peak Time: ----------------------------

Finish Time: --------------------------

Ascent Duration: ----------------------

Descent Duration: ---------------------

Total Time: ---------------------------

Total Distance Covered: ---------------

Weather Conditions:

Temperature: --------- ○ ○ ○ ○ ○ ○

Wind: ----------

(poor) (great)
Difficulty: ○ ○ ○ ○ ○ ○ ○ ○ ○

Fufillment: ○ ○ ○ ○ ○ ○ ○ ○ ○

Scenery: ○ ○ ○ ○ ○ ○ ○ ○ ○

Companions: -----------------

Notes/Photos:

Stob Ghabhar

Height: 1090m
Grid Ref: NN 23021 45506

Date: ----
Ascent Start Time: ----
Descent Start Time: ----
Peak Time: ----
Finish Time: ----
Ascent Duration: ----
Descent Duration: ----
Total Time: ----
Total Distance Covered: ----
Weather Conditions:
Temperature: ----
Wind: ----

(poor) (great)
Difficulty: ○ ○ ○ ○ ○ ○ ○ ○ ○
Fufillment: ○ ○ ○ ○ ○ ○ ○ ○ ○
Scenery: ○ ○ ○ ○ ○ ○ ○ ○ ○
Companions: ----

Notes/Photos:

Sgurr nan Clach Geala

Height: 1093m
Grid Ref: NH 16174 34229

Date: ....
Ascent Start Time: ....
Descent Start Time: ....
Peak Time: ....
Finish Time: ....
Ascent Duration: ....
Descent Duration: ....
Total Time: ....
Total Distance Covered: ....
Weather Conditions: ☀ ⛅ ☁ 🌧 🌬 ❄
Temperature: .... ○ ○ ○ ○ ○ ○
Wind: ....

(poor) (great)
Difficulty: ○ ○ ○ ○ ○ ○ ○ ○ ○ ○
Fufillment: ○ ○ ○ ○ ○ ○ ○ ○ ○ ○
Scenery: ○ ○ ○ ○ ○ ○ ○ ○ ○ ○
Companions: ....

....
....
....

Notes/Photos:

Sgurr Choinnich Mor

Height: 1094m
Grid Ref: NN 22774 71410

Date: ---------------------------------

Ascent Start Time: --------------------

Descent Start Time: -------------------

Peak Time: ----------------------------

Finish Time: --------------------------

Ascent Duration: ----------------------

Descent Duration: ---------------------

Total Time: ---------------------------

Total Distance Covered: ---------------

Weather Conditions:

Temperature: --------- ○ ○ ○ ○ ○ ○

Wind: -----------

(poor) (great)
Difficulty: ○ ○ ○ ○ ○ ○ ○ ○ ○

Fufillment: ○ ○ ○ ○ ○ ○ ○ ○ ○

Scenery: ○ ○ ○ ○ ○ ○ ○ ○ ○

Companions: -------------------

Notes/Photos:

Sgurr a'Mhaim

Height: 1099m
Grid Ref: NN 16469 66721

Date: ----------------------------------

Ascent Start Time: ---------------------

Descent Start Time: --------------------

Peak Time: -----------------------------

Finish Time: ---------------------------

Ascent Duration: -----------------------

Descent Duration: ----------------------

Total Time: ----------------------------

Total Distance Covered: ---------------

Weather Conditions: ☀ ⛅ ☁ 🌧 ⛆ ❄

Temperature: --------- ○ ○ ○ ○ ○ ○

Wind: -----------

(poor) (great)
Difficulty: ○ ○ ○ ○ ○ ○ ○ ○ ○

Fufillment: ○ ○ ○ ○ ○ ○ ○ ○ ○

Scenery: ○ ○ ○ ○ ○ ○ ○ ○ ○

Companions: ----------------

Notes/Photos:

Creise

Height: 1100m
Grid Ref: NN 23858 50636

Date: ----------------------------------

Ascent Start Time: --------------------

Descent Start Time: -------------------

Peak Time: ----------------------------

Finish Time: --------------------------

Ascent Duration: ----------------------

Descent Duration: ---------------------

Total Time: ---------------------------

Total Distance Covered: ---------------

Weather Conditions: ☀ ⛅ ☁ 🌧 🌦 ❄

Temperature: --------- ○ ○ ○ ○ ○ ○

Wind: ----------

(poor) (great)
Difficulty: ○ ○ ○ ○ ○ ○ ○ ○ ○

Fufillment: ○ ○ ○ ○ ○ ○ ○ ○ ○

Scenery: ○ ○ ○ ○ ○ ○ ○ ○ ○

Companions: --------------------

Notes/Photos:

Beinn Eibhinn

Height: 1102m
Grid Ref: NN 44968 73293

Date: ---------------------------------
Ascent Start Time: --------------------
Descent Start Time: -------------------
Peak Time: ----------------------------
Finish Time: --------------------------
Ascent Duration: ----------------------
Descent Duration: ---------------------
Total Time: ---------------------------
Total Distance Covered: ---------------
Weather Conditions:
Temperature: ---------
Wind: -----------

(poor) (great)
Difficulty: ○ ○ ○ ○ ○ ○ ○ ○ ○
Fufillment: ○ ○ ○ ○ ○ ○ ○ ○ ○
Scenery: ○ ○ ○ ○ ○ ○ ○ ○ ○
Companions: ----------------

Notes/Photos:

Mullach Fraoch-choire

Height: 1102m
Grid Ref: NH 09494 17142

Date: ----------------------------------

Ascent Start Time: --------------------

Descent Start Time: -------------------

Peak Time: ----------------------------

Finish Time: --------------------------

Ascent Duration: ----------------------

Descent Duration: ---------------------

Total Time: ---------------------------

Total Distance Covered: ---------------

Weather Conditions:

Temperature: _____ ○ ○ ○ ○ ○ ○

Wind: _____

(poor) (great)
Difficulty: ○ ○ ○ ○ ○ ○ ○ ○ ○ ○

Fufillment: ○ ○ ○ ○ ○ ○ ○ ○ ○ ○

Scenery: ○ ○ ○ ○ ○ ○ ○ ○ ○ ○

Companions: ------------------

Notes/Photos:

Beinn Ghlas

Height: 1103m
Grid Ref: NN 62531 40455

Date: _____

Ascent Start Time: _____

Descent Start Time: _____

Peak Time: _____

Finish Time: _____

Ascent Duration: _____

Descent Duration: _____

Total Time: _____

Total Distance Covered: _____

Weather Conditions: ☀ ⛅ ☁ 🌧 ⛈ ❄

Temperature: _____ ○ ○ ○ ○ ○ ○

Wind: _____

(poor) (great)
Difficulty: ○ ○ ○ ○ ○ ○ ○ ○ ○

Fufillment: ○ ○ ○ ○ ○ ○ ○ ○ ○

Scenery: ○ ○ ○ ○ ○ ○ ○ ○ ○

Companions: _____
_____
_____
_____

Notes/Photos:

Stob a'Choire Mheadhoin

Height: 1106m
Grid Ref: NN 31655 73634

Date: ---
Ascent Start Time: ---
Descent Start Time: ---
Peak Time: ---
Finish Time: ---
Ascent Duration: ---
Descent Duration: ---
Total Time: ---
Total Distance Covered: ---
Weather Conditions:
Temperature: ---
Wind: ---

(poor) (great)
Difficulty: ○ ○ ○ ○ ○ ○ ○ ○ ○
Fufillment: ○ ○ ○ ○ ○ ○ ○ ○ ○
Scenery: ○ ○ ○ ○ ○ ○ ○ ○ ○
Companions: ---

Notes/Photos:

Meall a'Bhuiridh

Height: 1108m
Grid Ref: NN 25066 50337

Date: ---------------------------------
Ascent Start Time: --------------------
Descent Start Time: -------------------
Peak Time: ----------------------------
Finish Time: --------------------------
Ascent Duration: ----------------------
Descent Duration: ---------------------
Total Time: ---------------------------
Total Distance Covered: ---------------
Weather Conditions: ☀ ⛅ ☁ 🌧 ❄ ❄
Temperature: --------- ○ ○ ○ ○ ○ ○
Wind: ----------

(poor) (great)
Difficulty: ○ ○ ○ ○ ○ ○ ○ ○ ○
Fufillment: ○ ○ ○ ○ ○ ○ ○ ○ ○
Scenery: ○ ○ ○ ○ ○ ○ ○ ○ ○
Companions: -----------------

Notes/Photos:

Sgurr nan Conbhairean

Height: 1109m
Grid Ref: NH 12991 13885

Date: ----------------------------------

Ascent Start Time: --------------------

Descent Start Time: -------------------

Peak Time: ----------------------------

Finish Time: --------------------------

Ascent Duration: ----------------------

Descent Duration: ---------------------

Total Time: ---------------------------

Total Distance Covered: ---------------

Weather Conditions:

Temperature: ------

Wind: ----------

(poor) (great)
Difficulty: ○ ○ ○ ○ ○ ○ ○ ○ ○

Fufillment: ○ ○ ○ ○ ○ ○ ○ ○ ○

Scenery: ○ ○ ○ ○ ○ ○ ○ ○ ○

Companions: --------------------

Notes/Photos:

Carn a'Choire Bhoidheach

Height: 1110m
Grid Ref: NO 22673 84548

Date: ----------------------------------
Ascent Start Time: --------------------
Descent Start Time: -------------------
Peak Time: ----------------------------
Finish Time: --------------------------
Ascent Duration: ----------------------
Descent Duration: ---------------------
Total Time: ---------------------------
Total Distance Covered: ---------------
Weather Conditions: ☀ ⛅ ☁ 🌧 🌦 ❄
Temperature: --------- ○ ○ ○ ○ ○ ○
Wind: -----------

(poor) (great)
Difficulty: ○ ○ ○ ○ ○ ○ ○ ○ ○
Fufillment: ○ ○ ○ ○ ○ ○ ○ ○ ○
Scenery: ○ ○ ○ ○ ○ ○ ○ ○ ○
Companions: -----------------

Notes/Photos:

Sgurr Mor

Height: 1112m
Grid Ref: NH 20325 71806

Date: ----------------------------------
Ascent Start Time: --------------------
Descent Start Time: -------------------
Peak Time: ----------------------------
Finish Time: --------------------------
Ascent Duration: ----------------------
Descent Duration: ---------------------
Total Time: ---------------------------
Total Distance Covered: ---------------
Weather Conditions:
Temperature: -------
Wind: ----------

(poor) (great)
Difficulty: ○ ○ ○ ○ ○ ○ ○ ○ ○ ○
Fufillment: ○ ○ ○ ○ ○ ○ ○ ○ ○ ○
Scenery: ○ ○ ○ ○ ○ ○ ○ ○ ○ ○
Companions: ----------------

Notes/Photos:

Tom a'Choinich

Height: 1113m
Grid Ref: NH 16405 27323

Date: -------------------------------
Ascent Start Time: --------------------
Descent Start Time: ------------------
Peak Time: ---------------------------
Finish Time: -------------------------
Ascent Duration: ---------------------
Descent Duration: --------------------
Total Time: --------------------------
Total Distance Covered: --------------
Weather Conditions:
Temperature: ---------
Wind: -----------

(poor) (great)
Difficulty: ○ ○ ○ ○ ○ ○ ○ ○ ○ ○
Fufillment: ○ ○ ○ ○ ○ ○ ○ ○ ○ ○
Scenery: ○ ○ ○ ○ ○ ○ ○ ○ ○ ○
Companions: ----------------

Notes/Photos:

Monadh Mor

Height: 1115m
Grid Ref: NN 93866 94207

Date: _____

Ascent Start Time: _____

Descent Start Time: _____

Peak Time: _____

Finish Time: _____

Ascent Duration: _____

Descent Duration: _____

Total Time: _____

Total Distance Covered: _____

Weather Conditions:

Temperature: _____ ○ ○ ○ ○ ○ ○

Wind: _____

(poor) (great)
Difficulty: ○ ○ ○ ○ ○ ○ ○ ○ ○

Fufillment: ○ ○ ○ ○ ○ ○ ○ ○ ○

Scenery: ○ ○ ○ ○ ○ ○ ○ ○ ○

Companions: _____

_____

_____

_____

Notes/Photos:

Stob Coire an Laoigh

Height: 1116m
Grid Ref: NN 23987 72523

Date: _____
Ascent Start Time: _____
Descent Start Time: _____
Peak Time: _____
Finish Time: _____
Ascent Duration: _____
Descent Duration: _____
Total Time: _____
Total Distance Covered: _____
Weather Conditions: ☀ ⛅ ☁ 🌧 🌦 ❄
Temperature: _____ ○ ○ ○ ○ ○ ○
Wind: _____

(poor) (great)
Difficulty: ○ ○ ○ ○ ○ ○ ○ ○ ○
Fufillment: ○ ○ ○ ○ ○ ○ ○ ○ ○
Scenery: ○ ○ ○ ○ ○ ○ ○ ○ ○
Companions: _____
_____
_____
_____

Notes/Photos:

Stob Coire Easain

Height: 1116m
Grid Ref: NN 30805 73057

Date: ------------------------------

Ascent Start Time: --------------------

Descent Start Time: ------------------

Peak Time: ---------------------------

Finish Time: -------------------------

Ascent Duration: ----------------------

Descent Duration: ---------------------

Total Time: --------------------------

Total Distance Covered: --------------

Weather Conditions:

Temperature: ---------

Wind: ----------

(poor) (great)
Difficulty: ○ ○ ○ ○ ○ ○ ○ ○ ○

Fufillment: ○ ○ ○ ○ ○ ○ ○ ○ ○

Scenery: ○ ○ ○ ○ ○ ○ ○ ○ ○

Companions: ----------------

Notes/Photos:

An Stuc
Height: 1118m
Grid Ref: NN 63892 43095

Date: ----------------------------------

Ascent Start Time: --------------------

Descent Start Time: -------------------

Peak Time: ---------------------------

Finish Time: --------------------------

Ascent Duration: ----------------------

Descent Duration: ---------------------

Total Time: ---------------------------

Total Distance Covered: --------------

Weather Conditions:

Temperature: --------- ○ ○ ○ ○ ○ ○

Wind: -----------

(poor) (great)
Difficulty: ○ ○ ○ ○ ○ ○ ○ ○ ○

Fufillment: ○ ○ ○ ○ ○ ○ ○ ○ ○

Scenery: ○ ○ ○ ○ ○ ○ ○ ○ ○

Companions: ------------------

Notes/Photos:

Meall Garbh

Height: 1118m
Grid Ref: NN 64439 43749

Date: ---
Ascent Start Time: ---
Descent Start Time: ---
Peak Time: ---
Finish Time: ---
Ascent Duration: ---
Descent Duration: ---
Total Time: ---
Total Distance Covered: ---
Weather Conditions:
Temperature: ---
Wind: ---

(poor) (great)
Difficulty: ○ ○ ○ ○ ○ ○ ○ ○ ○
Fufillment: ○ ○ ○ ○ ○ ○ ○ ○ ○
Scenery: ○ ○ ○ ○ ○ ○ ○ ○ ○
Companions: ---

Notes/Photos:

Sgor Gaoith

Height: 1118m
Grid Ref: NN 90301 98952

Date: _____

Ascent Start Time: _____

Descent Start Time: _____

Peak Time: _____

Finish Time: _____

Ascent Duration: _____

Descent Duration: _____

Total Time: _____

Total Distance Covered: _____

Weather Conditions:

Temperature: ○ ○ ○ ○ ○ ○

Wind: _____

(poor) (great)
Difficulty: ○ ○ ○ ○ ○ ○ ○ ○ ○

Fufillment: ○ ○ ○ ○ ○ ○ ○ ○ ○

Scenery: ○ ○ ○ ○ ○ ○ ○ ○ ○

Companions: _____

_____

_____

_____

Notes/Photos:

Aonach Beag

Height: 1118m
Grid Ref: NN 45789 74181

Date: ---------------------------------
Ascent Start Time: --------------------
Descent Start Time: -------------------
Peak Time: ----------------------------
Finish Time: --------------------------
Ascent Duration: ----------------------
Descent Duration: ---------------------
Total Time: ---------------------------
Total Distance Covered: ---------------
Weather Conditions:
Temperature: ---------
Wind: ----------

(poor) (great)
Difficulty: ○ ○ ○ ○ ○ ○ ○ ○ ○
Fufillment: ○ ○ ○ ○ ○ ○ ○ ○ ○
Scenery: ○ ○ ○ ○ ○ ○ ○ ○ ○
Companions: -------------------

Notes/Photos:

A'Chraileag

Height: 1120m
Grid Ref: NH 09434 14787

Date: ---
Ascent Start Time: ---
Descent Start Time: ---
Peak Time: ---
Finish Time: ---
Ascent Duration: ---
Descent Duration: ---
Total Time: ---
Total Distance Covered: ---
Weather Conditions:
Temperature:
Wind: ---

(poor) (great)
Difficulty: ○ ○ ○ ○ ○ ○ ○ ○ ○
Fufillment: ○ ○ ○ ○ ○ ○ ○ ○ ○
Scenery: ○ ○ ○ ○ ○ ○ ○ ○ ○
Companions: ---

Notes/Photos:

Ben Cruachan
Height: 1126m
Grid Ref: NN 06966 30464

Date: _____
Ascent Start Time: _____
Descent Start Time: _____
Peak Time: _____
Finish Time: _____
Ascent Duration: _____
Descent Duration: _____
Total Time: _____
Total Distance Covered: _____
Weather Conditions: ☀ ⛅ ☁ 🌧 ⛈ ❄
Temperature: _____ ○ ○ ○ ○ ○ ○
Wind: _____

(poor) (great)
Difficulty: ○ ○ ○ ○ ○ ○ ○ ○ ○
Fufillment: ○ ○ ○ ○ ○ ○ ○ ○ ○
Scenery: ○ ○ ○ ○ ○ ○ ○ ○ ○
Companions: _____
_____
_____
_____

Notes/Photos:

Beinn a'Ghlo - Carn nan Gabhar

Height: 1129m
Grid Ref: NN 97117 73305

Date: _____

Ascent Start Time: _____

Descent Start Time: _____

Peak Time: _____

Finish Time: _____

Ascent Duration: _____

Descent Duration: _____

Total Time: _____

Total Distance Covered: _____

Weather Conditions: ☀ ⛅ ☁ 🌦 🌧 ❄

Temperature: _____ ○ ○ ○ ○ ○ ○

Wind: _____

(poor) (great)
Difficulty: ○ ○ ○ ○ ○ ○ ○ ○ ○

Fufillment: ○ ○ ○ ○ ○ ○ ○ ○ ○

Scenery: ○ ○ ○ ○ ○ ○ ○ ○ ○

Companions: _____

_____

_____

_____

Notes/Photos:

Creag Meagaidh

Height: 1129m
Grid Ref: NN 41842 87536

Date: ----------------------------------

Ascent Start Time: ---------------------

Descent Start Time: --------------------

Peak Time: ------------------------------

Finish Time: ----------------------------

Ascent Duration: ------------------------

Descent Duration: -----------------------

Total Time: ------------------------------

Total Distance Covered: ----------------

Weather Conditions:

Temperature: _____ ○ ○ ○ ○ ○ ○

Wind: _____

(poor) (great)
Difficulty: ○ ○ ○ ○ ○ ○ ○ ○ ○

Fufillment: ○ ○ ○ ○ ○ ○ ○ ○ ○

Scenery: ○ ○ ○ ○ ○ ○ ○ ○ ○

Companions: ----------------

Notes/Photos:

Ben Lui
Height: 1130m
Grid Ref: NN 26639 26288

Date: ----------------------------------

Ascent Start Time: --------------------

Descent Start Time: -------------------

Peak Time: ----------------------------

Finish Time: --------------------------

Ascent Duration: ----------------------

Descent Duration: ---------------------

Total Time: ---------------------------

Total Distance Covered: ---------------

Weather Conditions:

Temperature: --------- ○ ○ ○ ○ ○ ○

Wind: ----------

(poor) (great)
Difficulty: ○ ○ ○ ○ ○ ○ ○ ○ ○ ○

Fufillment: ○ ○ ○ ○ ○ ○ ○ ○ ○ ○

Scenery: ○ ○ ○ ○ ○ ○ ○ ○ ○ ○

Companions: ------------------

Notes/Photos:

Binnein Mor

Height: 1130m
Grid Ref: NN 21222 66343

Date: ----------------------------------

Ascent Start Time: --------------------

Descent Start Time: -------------------

Peak Time: ----------------------------

Finish Time: ---------------------------

Ascent Duration: ----------------------

Descent Duration: ---------------------

Total Time: ----------------------------

Total Distance Covered: ---------------

Weather Conditions: ☀ ⛅ ☁ 🌧 ⛈ ❄

Temperature: --------- ○ ○ ○ ○ ○ ○

Wind: ----------

(poor)　　　　　　(great)
Difficulty: ○ ○ ○ ○ ○ ○ ○ ○ ○

Fufillment: ○ ○ ○ ○ ○ ○ ○ ○ ○

Scenery: ○ ○ ○ ○ ○ ○ ○ ○ ○

Companions: ----------------

Notes/Photos:

An Riabhachan

Height: 1130m
Grid Ref: NH 13366 34472

Date: ----------------------------------

Ascent Start Time: --------------------

Descent Start Time: -------------------

Peak Time: ----------------------------

Finish Time: --------------------------

Ascent Duration: ----------------------

Descent Duration: ---------------------

Total Time: ---------------------------

Total Distance Covered: ---------------

Weather Conditions: ☀ ⛅ ☁ 🌧 ☂ ❄

Temperature: --------- ○ ○ ○ ○ ○ ○

Wind: -----------

(poor) (great)
Difficulty: ○ ○ ○ ○ ○ ○ ○ ○ ○

Fufillment: ○ ○ ○ ○ ○ ○ ○ ○ ○

Scenery: ○ ○ ○ ○ ○ ○ ○ ○ ○

Companions: ----------------

Notes/Photos:

Geal-charn

Height: 1132m
Grid Ref: NN 46995 74620

Date: ----------------------------------
Ascent Start Time: --------------------
Descent Start Time: -------------------
Peak Time: ----------------------------
Finish Time: --------------------------
Ascent Duration: ----------------------
Descent Duration: ---------------------
Total Time: ---------------------------
Total Distance Covered: ---------------
Weather Conditions:
Temperature: --------- ○ ○ ○ ○ ○ ○
Wind: ----------

(poor) (great)
Difficulty: ○ ○ ○ ○ ○ ○ ○ ○ ○ ○
Fufillment: ○ ○ ○ ○ ○ ○ ○ ○ ○ ○
Scenery: ○ ○ ○ ○ ○ ○ ○ ○ ○ ○
Companions: ---------------

Notes/Photos:

Ben Alder

Height: 1148m
Grid Ref: NN 49619 71846

Date: ------------------------------------
Ascent Start Time: ----------------------
Descent Start Time: ---------------------
Peak Time: ------------------------------
Finish Time: ----------------------------
Ascent Duration: ------------------------
Descent Duration: -----------------------
Total Time: -----------------------------
Total Distance Covered: -----------------
Weather Conditions: ☀ ⛅ ☁ 🌧 ⛈ ❄
Temperature: ---------- ○ ○ ○ ○ ○ ○
Wind: -----------

Difficulty: (poor) ○ ○ ○ ○ ○ ○ ○ ○ ○ (great)
Fufillment: ○ ○ ○ ○ ○ ○ ○ ○ ○
Scenery: ○ ○ ○ ○ ○ ○ ○ ○ ○
Companions: ----------------

Notes/Photos:

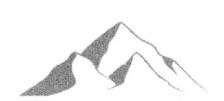

Bidean nam Bian

Height: 1150m
Grid Ref: NN 14345 54202

Date: ---
Ascent Start Time: ---
Descent Start Time: ---
Peak Time: ---
Finish Time: ---
Ascent Duration: ---
Descent Duration: ---
Total Time: ---
Total Distance Covered: ---
Weather Conditions:
Temperature: ---
Wind: ---

(poor) (great)
Difficulty: ○ ○ ○ ○ ○ ○ ○ ○ ○ ○
Fufillment: ○ ○ ○ ○ ○ ○ ○ ○ ○ ○
Scenery: ○ ○ ○ ○ ○ ○ ○ ○ ○ ○
Companions: ---

Notes/Photos:

Sgurr na Lapaich

Height: 1150m
Grid Ref: NH 15418 24382

Date: ----------------------------------

Ascent Start Time: ---------------------

Descent Start Time: -------------------

Peak Time: ------------------------------

Finish Time: ----------------------------

Ascent Duration: ------------------------

Descent Duration: -----------------------

Total Time: -----------------------------

Total Distance Covered: -----------------

Weather Conditions: ☀️ ⛅ ☁️ 🌧️ 🌦️ ❄️

Temperature: --------- ○ ○ ○ ○ ○ ○

Wind: -----------

(poor) (great)
Difficulty: ○ ○ ○ ○ ○ ○ ○ ○ ○ ○

Fufillment: ○ ○ ○ ○ ○ ○ ○ ○ ○ ○

Scenery: ○ ○ ○ ○ ○ ○ ○ ○ ○ ○

Companions: ---------------

Notes/Photos:

Sgurr nan Ceathreamhnan

Height: 1151m
Grid Ref: NH 05705 22840

Date: _____

Ascent Start Time: _____

Descent Start Time: _____

Peak Time: _____

Finish Time: _____

Ascent Duration: _____

Descent Duration: _____

Total Time: _____

Total Distance Covered: _____

Weather Conditions:

Temperature: _____ ○ ○ ○ ○ ○ ○

Wind: _____

(poor) (great)
Difficulty: ○ ○ ○ ○ ○ ○ ○ ○ ○ ○

Fufillment: ○ ○ ○ ○ ○ ○ ○ ○ ○ ○

Scenery: ○ ○ ○ ○ ○ ○ ○ ○ ○ ○

Companions: _____

_____

_____

_____

Notes/Photos:

Derry Cairngorm

Height: 1155m
Grid Ref: NO 01735 98023

Date: ----------------------------------

Ascent Start Time: ---------------------

Descent Start Time: --------------------

Peak Time: -----------------------------

Finish Time: ---------------------------

Ascent Duration: -----------------------

Descent Duration: ----------------------

Total Time: ----------------------------

Total Distance Covered: ----------------

Weather Conditions: ☀ ⛅ ☁ 🌧 🌦 ❄

Temperature: --------- ○ ○ ○ ○ ○ ○

Wind: ----------

(poor) (great)
Difficulty: ○ ○ ○ ○ ○ ○ ○ ○ ○ ○

Fufillment: ○ ○ ○ ○ ○ ○ ○ ○ ○ ○

Scenery: ○ ○ ○ ○ ○ ○ ○ ○ ○ ○

Companions: ----------------

Notes/Photos:

Lochnagar - Cac Carn Beag

Height: 1155m
Grid Ref: NO 24372 86131

Date: ------------------------------

Ascent Start Time: --------------------

Descent Start Time: -------------------

Peak Time: ----------------------

Finish Time: --------------------------

Ascent Duration: ----------------------

Descent Duration: --------------------

Total Time: -----------------------

Total Distance Covered: --------------

Weather Conditions:

Temperature: ---------

Wind: ----------

(poor) (great)
Difficulty: ○ ○ ○ ○ ○ ○ ○ ○ ○

Fufillment: ○ ○ ○ ○ ○ ○ ○ ○ ○

Scenery: ○ ○ ○ ○ ○ ○ ○ ○ ○

Companions: ----------------

Notes/Photos:

Beinn Bhrotain

Height: 1157m
Grid Ref: NN 95414 92283

Date: ....

Ascent Start Time: ....

Descent Start Time: ....

Peak Time: ....

Finish Time: ....

Ascent Duration: ....

Descent Duration: ....

Total Time: ....

Total Distance Covered: ....

Weather Conditions: ☀ ⛅ ☁ 🌧 ⛈ ❄

Temperature: .... ○ ○ ○ ○ ○ ○

Wind: ....

(poor) (great)
Difficulty: ○ ○ ○ ○ ○ ○ ○ ○ ○

Fufillment: ○ ○ ○ ○ ○ ○ ○ ○ ○

Scenery: ○ ○ ○ ○ ○ ○ ○ ○ ○

Companions: ....

....

....

....

Notes/Photos:

Stob Binnein

Height: 1165m
Grid Ref: NN 43484 22704

Date: ----------------------------------

Ascent Start Time: --------------------

Descent Start Time: -------------------

Peak Time: -----------------------------

Finish Time: ---------------------------

Ascent Duration: -----------------------

Descent Duration: ----------------------

Total Time: ----------------------------

Total Distance Covered: ---------------

Weather Conditions:

Temperature: --------- ○ ○ ○ ○ ○ ○

Wind: ----------

(poor) (great)
Difficulty: ○ ○ ○ ○ ○ ○ ○ ○ ○ ○

Fufillment: ○ ○ ○ ○ ○ ○ ○ ○ ○ ○

Scenery: ○ ○ ○ ○ ○ ○ ○ ○ ○ ○

Companions: --------------------

Notes/Photos:

Ben Avon

Height: 1171m
Grid Ref: NJ 13194 01836

Date: ----------------------------------

Ascent Start Time: ---------------------

Descent Start Time: -------------------

Peak Time: -----------------------------

Finish Time: ---------------------------

Ascent Duration: -----------------------

Descent Duration: ----------------------

Total Time: ----------------------------

Total Distance Covered: ---------------

Weather Conditions: ☼ ⛅ ☁ 🌧 🌦 ❄

Temperature: -------- ○ ○ ○ ○ ○ ○

Wind: -----------

(poor) (great)
Difficulty: ○ ○ ○ ○ ○ ○ ○ ○ ○ ○

Fufillment: ○ ○ ○ ○ ○ ○ ○ ○ ○ ○

Scenery: ○ ○ ○ ○ ○ ○ ○ ○ ○ ○

Companions: ----------------

Notes/Photos:

Ben More
Height: 1174m
Grid Ref: NN 43279 24409

Date: ----------------------------------

Ascent Start Time: -------------------

Descent Start Time: ------------------

Peak Time: -------------------------

Finish Time: -----------------------

Ascent Duration: ----------------------

Descent Duration: --------------------

Total Time: -------------------------

Total Distance Covered: --------------

Weather Conditions:

Temperature: ---------

Wind: ----------

(poor) (great)
Difficulty: ○ ○ ○ ○ ○ ○ ○ ○ ○ ○

Fufillment: ○ ○ ○ ○ ○ ○ ○ ○ ○ ○

Scenery: ○ ○ ○ ○ ○ ○ ○ ○ ○ ○

Companions: ------------------

Notes/Photos:

Stob Choire Claurigh

Height: 1177m
Grid Ref: NN 26199 73869

Date: ----------------------------------

Ascent Start Time: --------------------

Descent Start Time: -------------------

Peak Time: ---------------------------

Finish Time: --------------------------

Ascent Duration: ----------------------

Descent Duration: ---------------------

Total Time: ---------------------------

Total Distance Covered: --------------

Weather Conditions: ☼ ⛅ ☁ 🌧 🌦 ❄

Temperature: --------- ○ ○ ○ ○ ○ ○

Wind: -----------

(poor) (great)
Difficulty: ○ ○ ○ ○ ○ ○ ○ ○ ○

Fufillment: ○ ○ ○ ○ ○ ○ ○ ○ ○

Scenery: ○ ○ ○ ○ ○ ○ ○ ○ ○

Companions: ----------------

Notes/Photos:

Mam Sodhail

Height: 1181m
Grid Ref: NH 12010 25321

Date: ---------------------------------

Ascent Start Time: --------------------

Descent Start Time: -------------------

Peak Time: ---------------------------

Finish Time: -------------------------

Ascent Duration: ----------------------

Descent Duration: ---------------------

Total Time: --------------------------

Total Distance Covered: ---------------

Weather Conditions:

Temperature: ---------

Wind: ----------

(poor) (great)
Difficulty: ○ ○ ○ ○ ○ ○ ○ ○ ○

Fufillment: ○ ○ ○ ○ ○ ○ ○ ○ ○

Scenery: ○ ○ ○ ○ ○ ○ ○ ○ ○

Companions: ------------------

Notes/Photos:

Beinn Mheadhoin

Height: 1182m
Grid Ref: NJ 02461 01686

Date: ----------------------------------

Ascent Start Time: ---------------------

Descent Start Time: --------------------

Peak Time: -----------------------------

Finish Time: ---------------------------

Ascent Duration: -----------------------

Descent Duration: ----------------------

Total Time: ----------------------------

Total Distance Covered: ---------------

Weather Conditions: ☀ ⛅ ☁ 🌧 🌦 ❄

Temperature: --------- ○ ○ ○ ○ ○ ○

Wind: -----------

(poor) (great)
Difficulty: ○ ○ ○ ○ ○ ○ ○ ○ ○

Fufillment: ○ ○ ○ ○ ○ ○ ○ ○ ○

Scenery: ○ ○ ○ ○ ○ ○ ○ ○ ○

Companions: ------------------

Notes/Photos:

Carn Eige
Height: 1183m
Grid Ref: NH 12358 26186

Date: ---

Ascent Start Time: ---

Descent Start Time: ---

Peak Time: ---

Finish Time: ---

Ascent Duration: ---

Descent Duration: ---

Total Time: ---

Total Distance Covered: ---

Weather Conditions:

Temperature: ---

Wind: ---

(poor) (great)
Difficulty: ○ ○ ○ ○ ○ ○ ○ ○ ○ ○

Fufillment: ○ ○ ○ ○ ○ ○ ○ ○ ○ ○

Scenery: ○ ○ ○ ○ ○ ○ ○ ○ ○ ○

Companions: ---

Notes/Photos:

Beinn a'Bhuird

Height: 1197m
Grid Ref: NJ 09232 00612

Date: ----------------------------------
Ascent Start Time: ---------------------
Descent Start Time: --------------------
Peak Time: -----------------------------
Finish Time: ---------------------------
Ascent Duration: -----------------------
Descent Duration: ----------------------
Total Time: ----------------------------
Total Distance Covered: ----------------
Weather Conditions:
Temperature: ---------
Wind: ----------

Difficulty: (poor) ○ ○ ○ ○ ○ ○ ○ ○ ○ ○ (great)
Fufillment: ○ ○ ○ ○ ○ ○ ○ ○ ○ ○
Scenery: ○ ○ ○ ○ ○ ○ ○ ○ ○ ○
Companions: ----------------

Notes/Photos:

Ben Lawers

Height: 1214m
Grid Ref: NN 63555 41416

Date: ----------------------------------

Ascent Start Time: --------------------

Descent Start Time: -------------------

Peak Time: ----------------------------

Finish Time: --------------------------

Ascent Duration: ----------------------

Descent Duration: ---------------------

Total Time: ---------------------------

Total Distance Covered: ---------------

Weather Conditions: ☀ ⛅ ☁ 🌧 ⛈ ❄

Temperature: --------- ○ ○ ○ ○ ○ ○

Wind: ----------

(poor) (great)
Difficulty: ○ ○ ○ ○ ○ ○ ○ ○ ○

Fufillment: ○ ○ ○ ○ ○ ○ ○ ○ ○

Scenery: ○ ○ ○ ○ ○ ○ ○ ○ ○

Companions: -------------------

Notes/Photos:

Carn Mor Dearg

Height: 1220m
Grid Ref: NN 17752 72163

Date: ----------------------------------
Ascent Start Time: ---------------------
Descent Start Time: --------------------
Peak Time: -----------------------------
Finish Time: ---------------------------
Ascent Duration: -----------------------
Descent Duration: ----------------------
Total Time: ----------------------------
Total Distance Covered: ----------------
Weather Conditions: ☀ ⛅ ☁ 🌧 ☂ ❄
Temperature: --------- ○ ○ ○ ○ ○ ○
Wind: -----------

(poor) (great)
Difficulty: ○ ○ ○ ○ ○ ○ ○ ○ ○ ○
Fufillment: ○ ○ ○ ○ ○ ○ ○ ○ ○ ○
Scenery: ○ ○ ○ ○ ○ ○ ○ ○ ○ ○
Companions: ---------------

Notes/Photos:

Aonach Mor

Height: 1221m
Grid Ref: NN 19309 72953

Date: ----------------------------------
Ascent Start Time: --------------------
Descent Start Time: -------------------
Peak Time: ----------------------------
Finish Time: --------------------------
Ascent Duration: ----------------------
Descent Duration: ---------------------
Total Time: ---------------------------
Total Distance Covered: ---------------
Weather Conditions:
Temperature: ---------
Wind: ----------

(poor) (great)
Difficulty: ○ ○ ○ ○ ○ ○ ○ ○ ○
Fufillment: ○ ○ ○ ○ ○ ○ ○ ○ ○
Scenery: ○ ○ ○ ○ ○ ○ ○ ○ ○
Companions: --------------------

Notes/Photos:

Aonach Beag
Height: 1234m
Grid Ref: NN 19710 71493

Date: ....

Ascent Start Time: ....

Descent Start Time: ....

Peak Time: ....

Finish Time: ....

Ascent Duration: ....

Descent Duration: ....

Total Time: ....

Total Distance Covered: ....

Weather Conditions: ☀ ⛅ ☁ 🌧 ⛈ ❄

Temperature: .... ○ ○ ○ ○ ○ ○

Wind: ....

(poor) (great)
Difficulty: ○ ○ ○ ○ ○ ○ ○ ○ ○

Fufillment: ○ ○ ○ ○ ○ ○ ○ ○ ○

Scenery: ○ ○ ○ ○ ○ ○ ○ ○ ○

Companions: ....

....

....

....

Notes/Photos:

Cairn Gorm
Height: 1245m
Grid Ref: NJ 00517 04056

Date: ----------------------------------

Ascent Start Time: --------------------

Descent Start Time: -------------------

Peak Time: ------------------------------

Finish Time: ----------------------------

Ascent Duration: ------------------------

Descent Duration: -----------------------

Total Time: -----------------------------

Total Distance Covered: ----------------

Weather Conditions:

Temperature: ----------

Wind: -----------

(poor) (great)
Difficulty: ○ ○ ○ ○ ○ ○ ○ ○ ○ ○

Fulfillment: ○ ○ ○ ○ ○ ○ ○ ○ ○ ○

Scenery: ○ ○ ○ ○ ○ ○ ○ ○ ○ ○

Companions: ----------------

Notes/Photos:

Sgor an Lochain Uaine

Height: 1258m
Grid Ref: NN 95423 97684

Date: ---------------------------------
Ascent Start Time: --------------------
Descent Start Time: -------------------
Peak Time: ----------------------------
Finish Time: --------------------------
Ascent Duration: ----------------------
Descent Duration: ---------------------
Total Time: ---------------------------
Total Distance Covered: ---------------
Weather Conditions: ☼ ⛅ ☁ 🌧 🌦 ❄
Temperature: --------- ○ ○ ○ ○ ○ ○
Wind: ----------

(poor) (great)
Difficulty: ○ ○ ○ ○ ○ ○ ○ ○ ○
Fufillment: ○ ○ ○ ○ ○ ○ ○ ○ ○
Scenery: ○ ○ ○ ○ ○ ○ ○ ○ ○
Companions: ----------------

Notes/Photos:

Cairn Toul

Height: 1291m
Grid Ref: NN 96329 97220

Date: ------------------------------

Ascent Start Time: --------------------

Descent Start Time: -------------------

Peak Time: ---------------------------

Finish Time: -------------------------

Ascent Duration: ----------------------

Descent Duration: ---------------------

Total Time: --------------------------

Total Distance Covered: --------------

Weather Conditions:

Temperature: ---------

Wind: ----------

(poor) (great)
Difficulty: ○ ○ ○ ○ ○ ○ ○ ○ ○

Fufillment: ○ ○ ○ ○ ○ ○ ○ ○ ○

Scenery: ○ ○ ○ ○ ○ ○ ○ ○ ○

Companions: ------------------

Notes/Photos:

Braeriach

Height: 1296m
Grid Ref: NN 95329 99907

Date:	Difficulty: (poor) ○○○○○○○○○○ (great)
Ascent Start Time:	Fufillment: ○○○○○○○○○○
Descent Start Time:	Scenery: ○○○○○○○○○○
Peak Time:	Companions:
Finish Time:	
Ascent Duration:	
Descent Duration:	
Total Time:	

Total Distance Covered:

Weather Conditions: ☀ ⛅ ☁ 🌧 🌦 ❄

Temperature: ○ ○ ○ ○ ○ ○

Wind:

Notes/Photos:

Ben Macdui

Height: 1309m
Grid Ref: NN 98900 98934

Date: ----------------------------------

Ascent Start Time: --------------------

Descent Start Time: -------------------

Peak Time: ----------------------------

Finish Time: --------------------------

Ascent Duration: ----------------------

Descent Duration: ---------------------

Total Time: ---------------------------

Total Distance Covered: ---------------

Weather Conditions: ☀ ⛅ ☁ 🌧 ⛈ ❄

Temperature: _____ ○ ○ ○ ○ ○ ○

Wind: ----------

(poor) (great)
Difficulty: ○ ○ ○ ○ ○ ○ ○ ○ ○

Fufillment: ○ ○ ○ ○ ○ ○ ○ ○ ○

Scenery: ○ ○ ○ ○ ○ ○ ○ ○ ○

Companions: ----------------

Notes/Photos:

Forte William
2hr 38

PH33 6SQ

Ben Nevis
Height: 1344m
Grid Ref: NN 16670 71279

Date: ----
Ascent Start Time: ----
Descent Start Time: ----
Peak Time: ----
Finish Time: ----
Ascent Duration: ----
Descent Duration: ----
Total Time: ----
Total Distance Covered: ----
Weather Conditions: ☼ ⛅ ☁ 🌧 ⛈ ❄
Temperature: ---- ○ ○ ○ ○ ○ ○
Wind: ----

(poor) (great)
Difficulty: ○ ○ ○ ○ ○ ○ ○ ○ ○
Fufillment: ○ ○ ○ ○ ○ ○ ○ ○ ○
Scenery: ○ ○ ○ ○ ○ ○ ○ ○ ○
Companions: ----

Notes/Photos:

Notes

Notes

Printed in Great Britain
by Amazon